CAMBRIDGE
Primary Mathematics

Learner's Book 2

Cherri Moseley & Janet Rees

CAMBRIDGE
UNIVERSITY PRESS & ASSESSMENT

Shaftesbury Road, Cambridge CB2 8EA, United Kingdom

One Liberty Plaza, 20th Floor, New York, NY 10006, USA

477 Williamstown Road, Port Melbourne, VIC 3207, Australia

314–321, 3rd Floor, Plot 3, Splendor Forum, Jasola District Centre, New Delhi – 110025, India

103 Penang Road, #05–06/07, Visioncrest Commercial, Singapore 238467

Cambridge University Press & Assessment is a department of the University of Cambridge.

We share the University's mission to contribute to society through the pursuit of education, learning and research at the highest international levels of excellence.

www.cambridge.org
Information on this title: www.cambridge.org/9781108746441

© Cambridge University Press & Assessment 2021

This publication is in copyright. Subject to statutory exception and to the provisions of relevant collective licensing agreements, no reproduction of any part may take place without the written permission of Cambridge University Press & Assessment.

First published 2014
Second edition 2021

20 19 18 17 16 15

Printed in Dubai by Oriental Press

A catalogue record for this publication is available from the British Library

ISBN   978-1-108-74644-1   Learner's Book with Digital Access (1 Year)
ISBN   978-1-108-96412-8   Digital Learner's Book (1 Year)
ISBN   978-1-108-96411-1   Learner's Book eBook

Additional resources for this publication at www.cambridge.org/9781108746441

Cambridge University Press & Assessment has no responsibility for the persistence or accuracy of URLs for external or third-party internet websites referred to in this publication, and does not guarantee that any content on such websites is, or will remain, accurate or appropriate. Information regarding prices, travel timetables, and other factual information given in this work is correct at the time of first printing but Cambridge University Press & Assessment does not guarantee the accuracy of such information thereafter.

Projects and their accompanying teacher guidance have been written by the NRICH Team. NRICH is an innovative collaboration between the Faculties of Mathematics and Education at the University of Cambridge, which focuses on problem solving and on creating opportunities for students to learn mathematics through exploration and discussion https://nrich.maths.org.

NOTICE TO TEACHERS IN THE UK
It is illegal to reproduce any part of this work in material form (including photocopying and electronic storage) except under the following circumstances:
(i)   where you are abiding by a licence granted to your school or institution by the Copyright Licensing Agency;
(ii) where no such licence exists, or where you wish to exceed the terms of a licence, and you have gained the written permission of Cambridge University Press & Assessment;
(iii) where you are allowed to reproduce without permission under the provisions of Chapter 3 of the Copyright, Designs and Patents Act 1988, which covers, for example, the reproduction of short passages within certain types of educational anthology and reproduction for the purposes of setting examination questions.

Introduction

Welcome to Stage 2 of **Cambridge Primary Mathematics**. We hope this book will show you how interesting and exciting mathematics can be.

Mathematics is everywhere. Everyone uses mathematics every day. Where have you noticed mathematics?

Have you ever wondered about any of these questions?

- Counting lots of things one by one is slow and it's easy to make a mistake. Is there a better way?
- What makes a number odd or even?
- What are centimetres, metres, grams, kilograms, millilitres and litres?
- What is it that repeats in a repeating pattern?
- How do you use a calendar?
- How can I explain to someone how to get to my house?
- How do you solve a mathematics problem?

You will work like a mathematician to find the answers to some of these questions. It is good to talk about the mathematics as you explore, sharing ideas. You will reflect on what you did and how you did it, and think about whether you would do the same next time.

You will be able to practise new skills and check how you are doing and also challenge yourself to find out more. You will be able to make connections between what seem to be different areas of mathematics.

We hope you enjoy thinking and working like a mathematician.

Cherri Moseley and Janet Rees

Contents

Page	Unit		Maths strand
6	How to use this book		
8	Thinking and Working Mathematically		

10	1	Numbers to 100
		    1.1 Numbers to 100
		    1.2 Counting up to 100 objects
		    1.3 Comparing and ordering numbers
			Number

28	Project 1: Possibly odd		

29	2	Geometry
		    2.1 3D shapes
		    2.2 2D shape and symmetry
		    2.3 Fractions of shapes
			Geometry and measure

51	Project 2: Strange submarines		

52	3	Measures
		    3.1 Length
		    3.2 Drawing and measuring lines
			Geometry and measure

68	4	Statistics 4.1 Carroll diagrams and tally charts	Statistics and probability

79	5	Working with numbers to 100
		    5.1 Addition
		    5.2 Subtraction
		    5.3 Multiplication
		    5.4 Division
			Number

101	Project 3: Borrowing pencils		
102	6	Money 6.1 Money	Number
109	7	Time 7.1 Units of time and the calendar	Geometry and measure
115	Project 4: Time a task		

Contents

Page	Unit		Maths strand
116	8	Numbers to 100 (2)	Number
		8.1　Numbers in words, rounding and regrouping	
		8.2　Fractions of numbers	
128	9	Statistics (2)	Statistics and probability
		9.1　Venn diagrams, lists and tables	
		9.2　Pictograms and block graphs	
146	10	Calculating	Number
		10.1　Adding and subtracting two 2-digit numbers	
		10.2　Connecting addition and subtraction	
		10.3　Multiplication	
		10.4　Division	
168	Project 5: 100 square		
170	11	Geometry (2)	Geometry and measure
		11.1　Angles and turns	
		11.2　Circles	
182	12	Telling the time	Geometry and measure
		12.1　Telling the time	
193	13	Measures (2)	Geometry and measure
		13.1　Mass and temperature	
		13.2　Capacity	
209	Project 6: Sorting orange juice		
211	14	Pattern and probability	Statistics and probability
		14.1　Pattern and probability	
222	15	Symmetry, position and movement	Geometry and measure
		15.1　Symmetry, position and movement	
231	Glossary		
251	Acknowledgements		

How to use this book

In this book you will find lots of different features to help your learning.

Questions to find out what you know already.

> **Getting started**
> 1. Split each number into tens and ones.
>   84   37   65

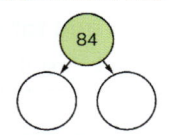

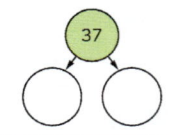

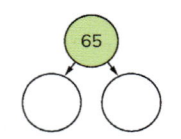

What you will learn in the unit.

> **We are going to ...**
> - say, read and write numbers from 0 to 100
> - know the value of each digit in a 2-digit number
> - count on and back in steps of 1 and 10 from any number.

Important words that you will use.

> column   digit   place holder
> representation   row

Step-by-step examples showing a way to solve a problem.

> **Worked example 3**
> A number sequence starts at 58.
> It counts back in twos and stops at 50.
> What are the numbers in this sequence? 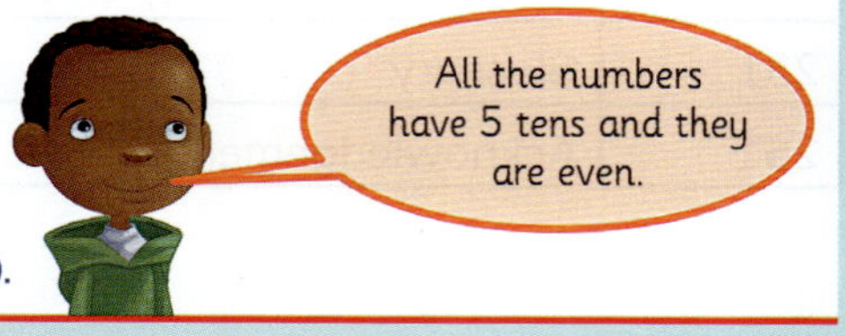
>
> *All the numbers have 5 tens and they are even.*
>
> **Answer:** 58, 56, 54, 52, 50.

There are often many different ways to solve a problem.

How to use this book

These questions will help you to develop your skills of thinking and working mathematically.

> 6 Compare 75 and 57.
> Which is the greater number?
> Use a place value chart or a number line to help you.
>
> 0 10 20 30 40 50 60 70 80 90 100

An investigation to carry out with a partner or in groups. This will help develop your skills of thinking and working mathematically.

Let's investigate

Zara draws this shape on the 100 square. She says she always has 2 or 3 odd numbers in her shape.

Is Zara correct?
Convince your partner that you are correct.

Questions to help you think about how you learn.

Compare with a partner how you each worked out the missing numbers in question 6.
What did you do the same?
What did you do differently?

What you have learned in the unit. Tick the column to show how you feel about each thing.

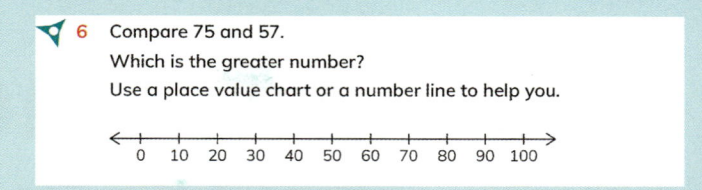

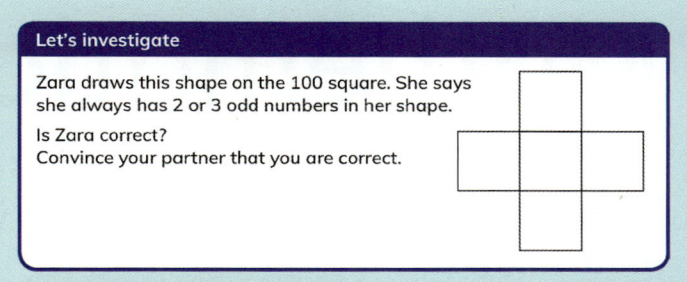

Look what I can do!

- I can represent 2-digit numbers in tens and ones.
- I can estimate how many there are then count to check.
- I can count on and back in ones, twos and tens.

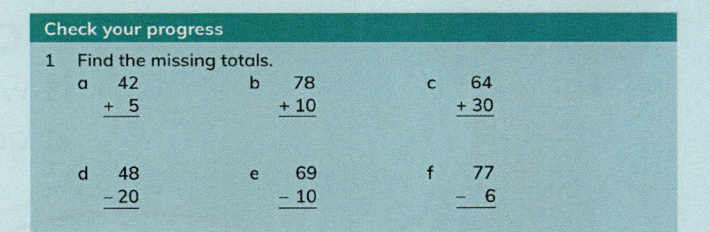

Questions that cover what you have learned in the unit.

Check your progress

1 Find the missing totals.

a	42	b	78	c	64
	+ 5		+ 10		+ 30

d	48	e	69	f	77
	− 20		− 10		− 6

At the end of several units, there is a project for you to carry out using what you have learned. You might make something or solve a problem.

> **Project 4**
>
> **Time a task**
>
> For this activity you will need to work in pairs.
>
> One of you will use a timer that shows seconds, and the other will choose one of the following tasks:
>
> a Counting to 20
> b Drawing a simple stick man
> c Standing on one foot for as long as possible
> d Saying a nursery rhyme
> e Walking slowly round the room

Projects and their accompanying teacher guidance have been written by the NRICH Team. NRICH is an innovative collaboration between the Faculties of Mathematics and Education at the University of Cambridge, which focuses on problem solving and on creating opportunities for students to learn mathematics through exploration and discussion.
https://nrich.maths.org

Thinking and Working Mathematically

There are some important skills that you will develop as you learn mathematics.

Specialising is when I test examples to see if they fit a rule or pattern.

Characterising is when I explain how a group of things are the same.

Generalising is when I can explain and use a rule or pattern to find more examples.

Classifying is when I put things into groups and can say what rule I have used.

Thinking and Working Mathematically

Critiquing is when I think about what is good and what could be better in my work or someone else's work.

Improving is when I try to make my maths better.

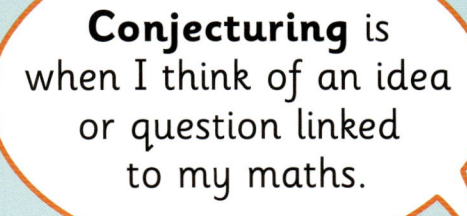

Conjecturing is when I think of an idea or question linked to my maths.

Convincing is when I explain my thinking to someone else, to help them understand.

1 ▶ Numbers to 100

Getting started

1   Add some facts about number fourteen.

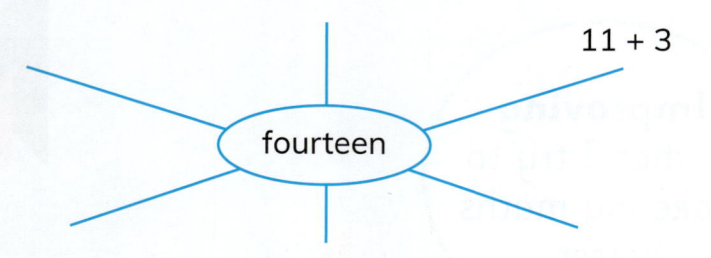

   11 + 3

   fourteen

2   Sort the numbers from 0 to 20 in the Venn diagram.

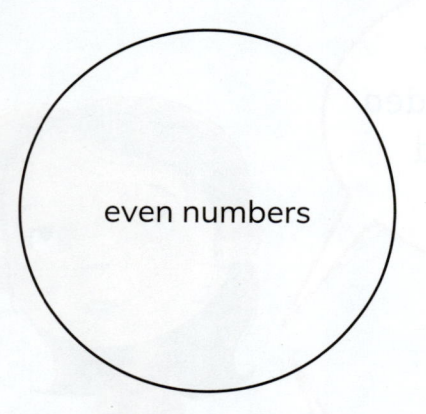

   even numbers

3   Show 18 on this number line.

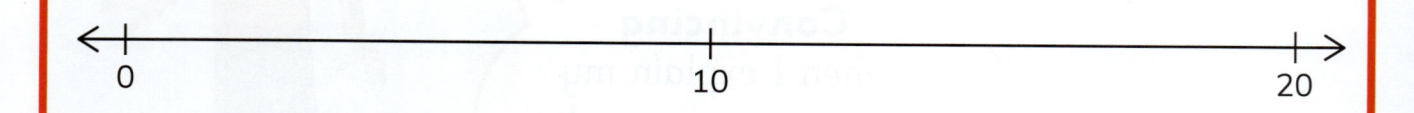

   0 — 10 — 20

1 Numbers to 100

In this unit you will explore numbers to 100.

You might live at number 47, read a book with 64 pages in it and have collected 71 stickers.

You use numbers every day, in many different ways.

1 Numbers to 100

> 1.1 Numbers to 100

We are going to ...
- say, read and write numbers from 0 to 100
- know the value of each digit in a 2-digit number
- count on and back in steps of 1 and 10 from any number.

There are many patterns to discover in the numbers to 100. You will find out how many tens and how many ones there are in each number to help you to understand the order of the numbers.

column   digit   place holder
representation   row

1	2	3	4	5	6	7	8	9	10
11	12	13	14	15	16	17	18	19	20
21	22	23	24	25	26	27	28	29	30
31	32	33	34	35	36	37	38	39	40
41	42	43	44	45	46	47	48	49	50
51	52	53	54	55	56	57	58	59	60
61	62	63	64	65	66	67	68	69	70
71	72	73	74	75	76	77	78	79	80
81	82	83	84	85	86	87	88	89	90
91	92	93	94	95	96	97	98	99	100

24
20   4

1.1 Numbers to 100

Exercise 1.1

1 Write the missing numbers.

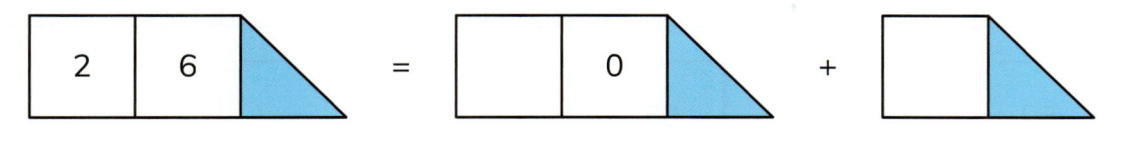

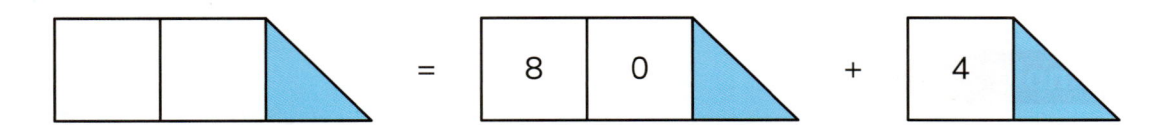

   | 2 | 6 | = | | 0 | + | |

   | | | = | 5 | 0 | + | 8 |

   | | | = | 8 | 0 | + | 4 |

> **Worked example 1**
>
> This is a row from the 100 square.
>
> | 21 | | | | 25 | | | | | 30 |
>
> Write the missing numbers.
>
> Count on in ones.
> 21, 22, 23, 24, 25.
>
> Count on in ones.
> 25, 26, 27, 28, 29, 30.
>
> Answer: | 21 | 22 | 23 | 24 | 25 | 26 | 27 | 28 | 29 | 30 |
>
> The ones change when I count. There are always two tens until I count to 30.

1 Numbers to 100

2 Write the missing numbers.

31				35					40

61	62			65					

				95					100

Worked example 2

This is a column from the 100 square.

Write the missing numbers.

Count on in tens. 2, 12, 22, 32, 42, 52, 62, 72, 82, 92. The tens change when I count. The number of ones stays the same.

2
12
92

Answer:

2
12
22
32
42
52
62
72
82
92

1.1 Numbers to 100

3. Write the missing numbers.

5	7	10
55	57	
		100

1 Numbers to 100

Let's investigate

1	2	3	4	5	6	7	8	9	10
11	12	13	14	15	16	17	18	19	20
21	22	23	24	25	26	27	28	29	30
31	32	33	34	35	36	37	38	39	40
41	42	43	44	45	46	47	48	49	50
51	52	53	54	55	56	57	58	59	60
61	62	63	64	65	66	67	68	69	70
71	72	73	74	75	76	77	78	79	80
81	82	83	84	85	86	87	88	89	90
91	92	93	94	95	96	97	98	99	100

How is every row in the 100 square the same?

How is every row different?

Talk about what you notice with your partner or in a small group.

1.1 Numbers to 100

4 Which 2-digit numbers are represented below?

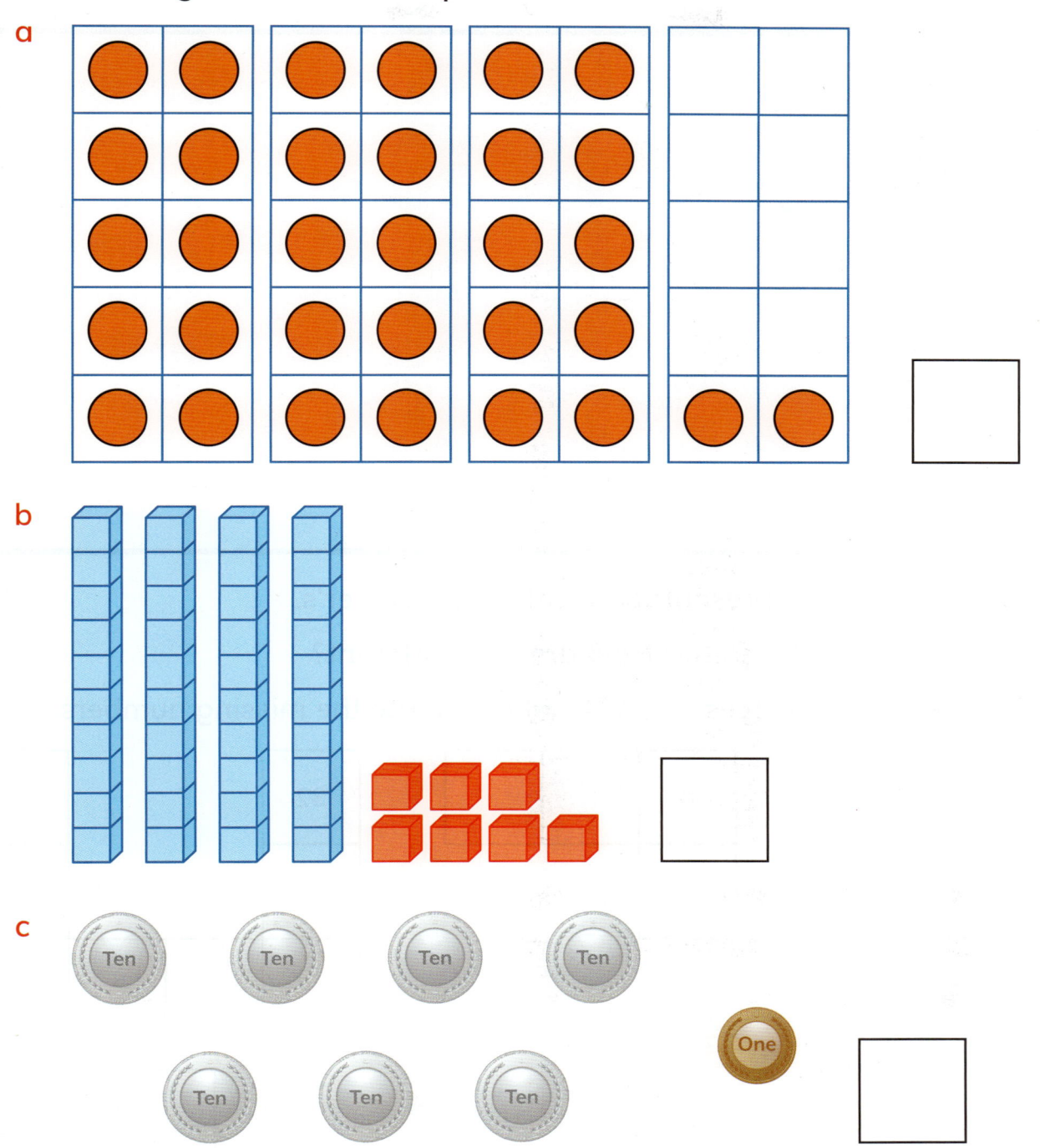

a

b

c

1 Numbers to 100

5   Draw a different representation of the number shown.

```
      53
     /  \
   50    3
```

Compare your representation with your partner's.

How are they the same? How are they different?

6   Here are some pieces of a 100 square. Write the missing numbers.

4

8

32

67

45

79

1.2 Counting up to 100 objects

> Compare with a partner how you each worked out the missing numbers in question 6.
> What did you do the same?
> What did you do differently?

Look what I can do!

- I can say, read and write numbers from 0 to 100.
- I can say and represent the value of each digit in a 2-digit number.
- I can count on and back in steps of 1 and 10 from any number, using the 100 square for support.

> 1.2 Counting up to 100 objects

We are going to ...

- represent 2-digit numbers in tens and ones
- estimate how many objects there are then count to check
- count on and back in ones, twos and tens.

Now that you know the order of the numbers to 100, you can use them to estimate how many objects there are and count them.

Counting in tens helps you to count larger collections quickly and accurately.

accurate, accurately
collection   order

19

1 Numbers to 100

Exercise 1.2

1

40	20	50
80	60	10
30	100	90

Which tens number is missing from the grid? _____

Write the tens numbers in order, from 10 to 100.

| 10 | | | | | | | | | 100 |

2   Arun and Zara make some numbers.

Arun chooses the tens. Zara chooses the ones.

Write each number they make in a part whole diagram.

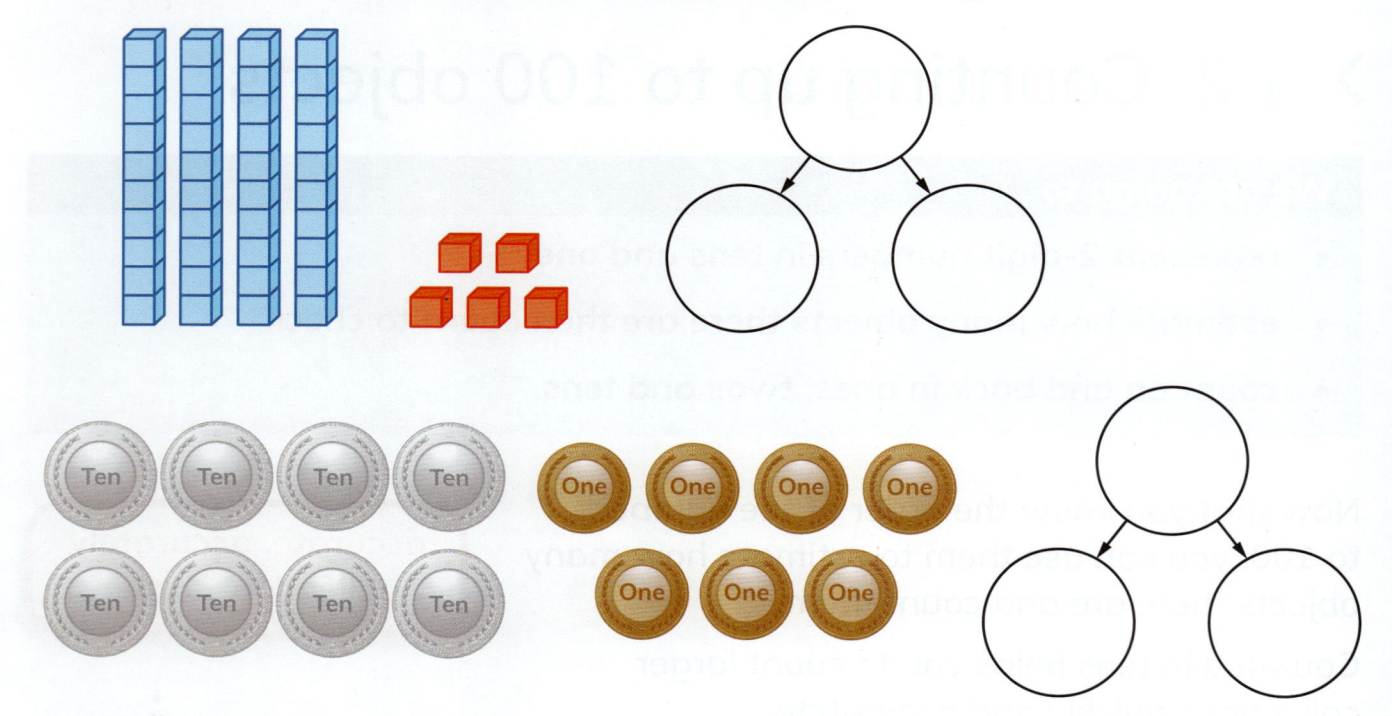

1.2 Counting up to 100 objects

> **Let's investigate**
>
> What if Zara chose zero ones?
>
> What can you say about those numbers?
>
> What if Arun chose zero tens?
>
> What can you say about those numbers?
>
> Discuss your answers with a partner.

3   How many in each collection? Estimate then count to check.

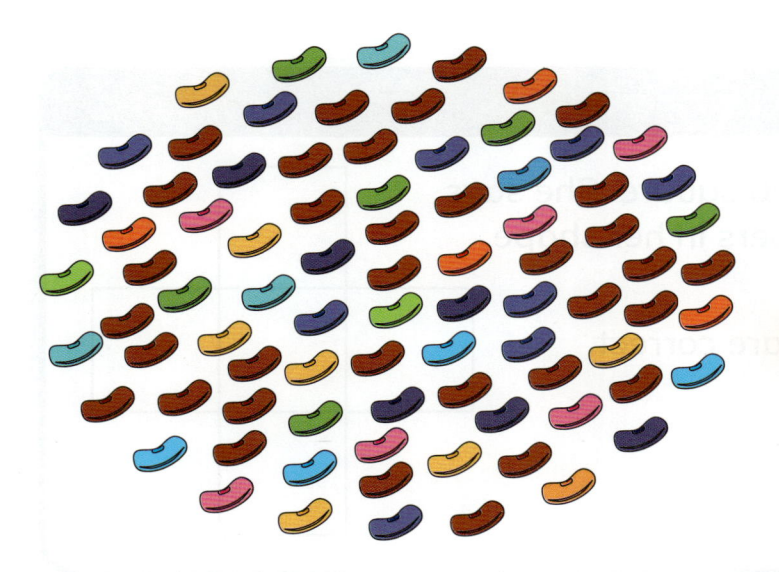

Estimate			
10	20	50	100
Count			

Tip

Draw a ring around groups of 10 objects. Count in tens and then in ones to find out how many in the collection.

Estimate			
10	20	50	100
Count			

Tip

You could choose to count in twos as well as tens.

21

1 Numbers to 100

> Were your estimates good in question 3?
> What helps you to make a good estimate?

4   Marcus counts from 0 to 100 in twos.

   Draw a ring around any numbers he does **not** say.

   68   7   24   42   37   91   15   86   59   63   8   11   73

   Why doesn't Marcus say these numbers?

Let's investigate

Zara draws this shape on the 100 square. She says she always has 2 or 3 odd numbers in her shape.

Is Zara correct?
Convince your partner that you are correct.

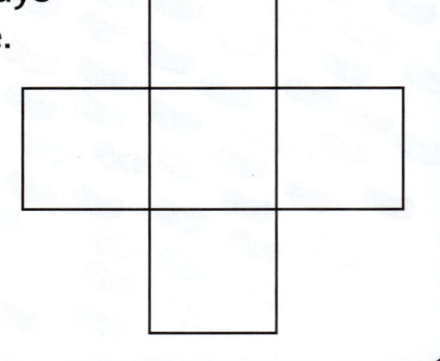

> How did you convince your partner that you were correct?
> Did your partner understand your thinking?

Look what I can do!

- I can represent 2-digit numbers in tens and ones.
- I can estimate how many there are then count to check.
- I can count on and back in ones, twos and tens.

> 1.3 Comparing and ordering numbers

> We are going to ...
> - use what you know about place value to compare and order numbers
> - make sequences of numbers
> - find out how to say and use ordinal numbers.

Now that you know about numbers to 100, you can use them to compare quantities.

36 is more than 24, so there are more marbles in the box of 36 marbles than in the bag of 24 marbles.

> close, closer
> extend a sequence
> ordering   ordinal numbers
> sequence

Exercise 1.3

1 Show 29, 65 and 82 on this number line.

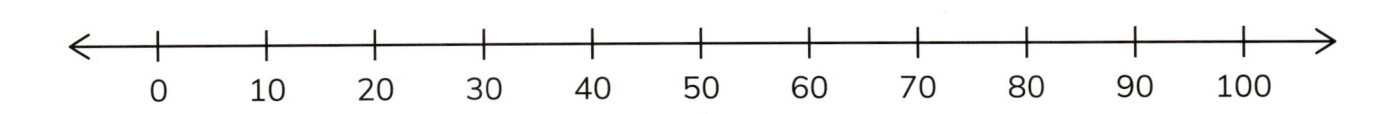

0 10 20 30 40 50 60 70 80 90 100

23

1 Numbers to 100

2   Use what you know about ordinal numbers to find each monster.
    Start at the bus stop. Draw a ring around the 2nd monster.
    Draw a line under the 6th monster.
    Tick the 3rd monster.

Worked example 3

A number sequence starts at 58.
It counts back in twos and stops at 50.
What are the numbers in this sequence?

All the numbers have 5 tens and they are even.

Answer: 58, 56, 54, 52, 50.

3   A number sequence starts at 37.
    It counts on in tens and stops at 77.
    What are the numbers in the sequence?

    _____   _____   _____   _____   _____

4   What can you say about all the numbers in the sequence
    you wrote for question 3?

1.3 Comparing and ordering numbers

5 Sofia's number sequence is 74, 64, 54, 44, 34.
   Complete the description of Sofia's number sequence.

   _____ at 74. Count _____ in tens. Stop at _____.

Worked example 4

Compare 34 and 43. Which is the greater number?

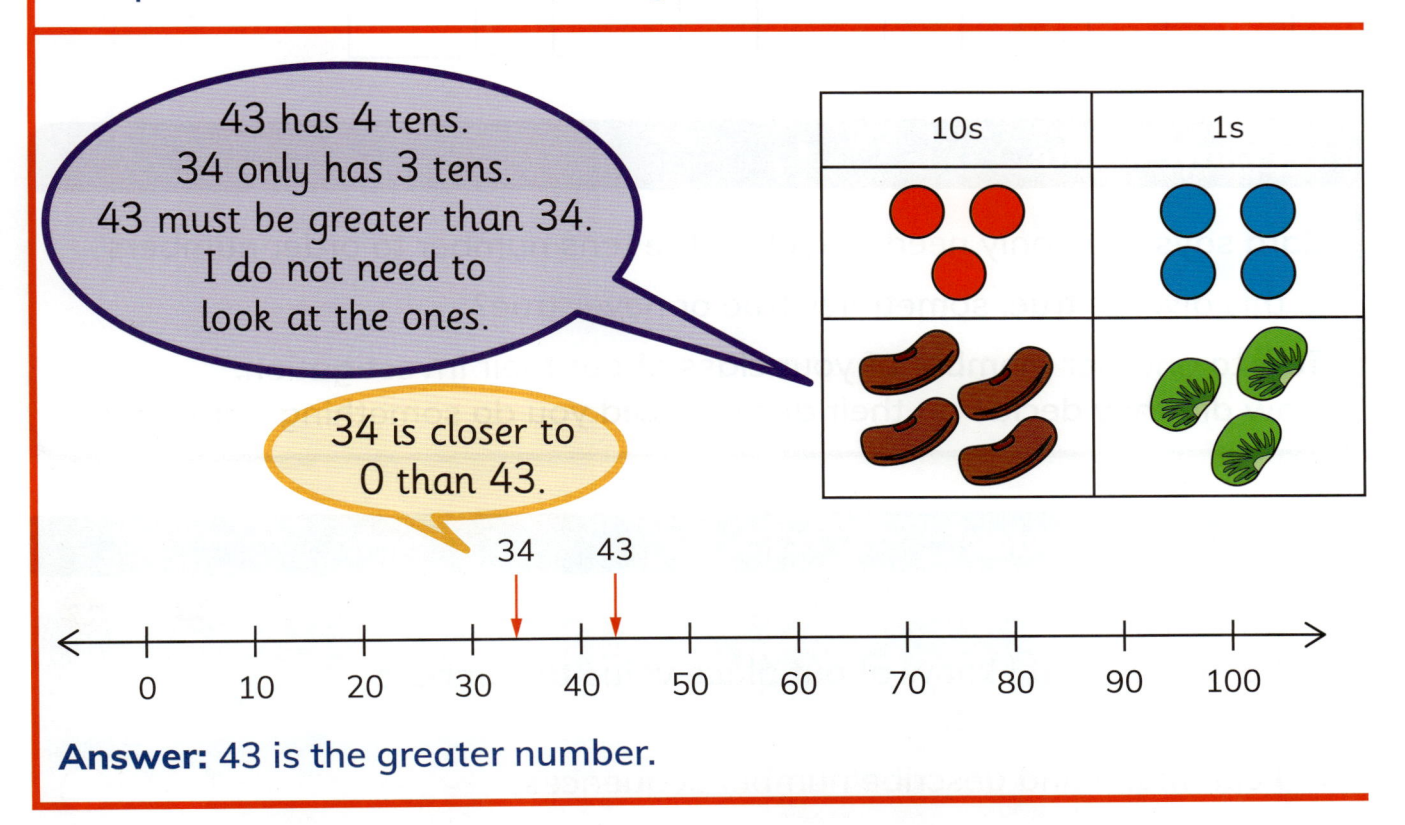

43 has 4 tens. 34 only has 3 tens. 43 must be greater than 34. I do not need to look at the ones.

34 is closer to 0 than 43.

Answer: 43 is the greater number.

6 Compare 75 and 57.

   Which is the greater number?

   Use a number line or place value grid to help you.

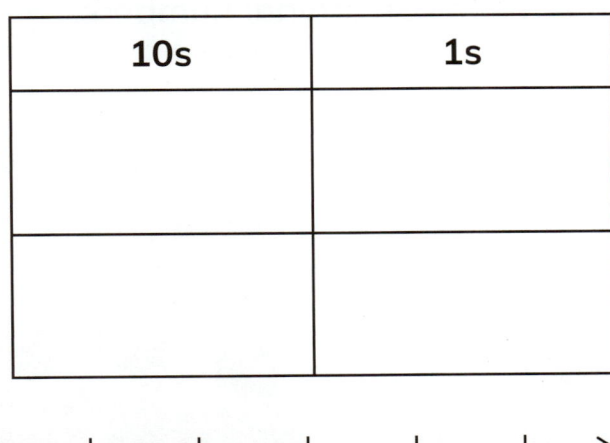

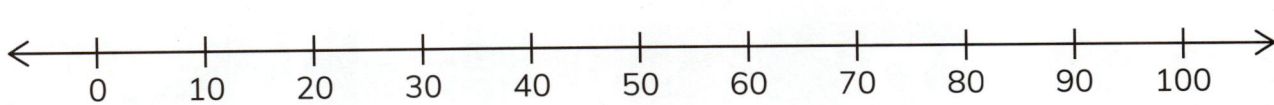

1 Numbers to 100

7 Order these numbers from smallest to greatest.

| 67 | 42 | 86 | 34 | 21 |

You could use a place value grid or a number line to help you.

☐ ☐ ☐ ☐ ☐

Let's investigate

Zara says, 'You only need to look at the tens number to order numbers'.

Is this always true, sometimes true or never true?

Talk to another member of your class about their investigation. How did they decide on their answer? Did you do something different?

Look what I can do!

- I can use what I know about place value to compare and order numbers.
- I can make and describe number sequences.
- I can use ordinal numbers.

1.3 Comparing and ordering numbers

Check your progress

1. Complete the missing numbers on these pieces from the 100 square.

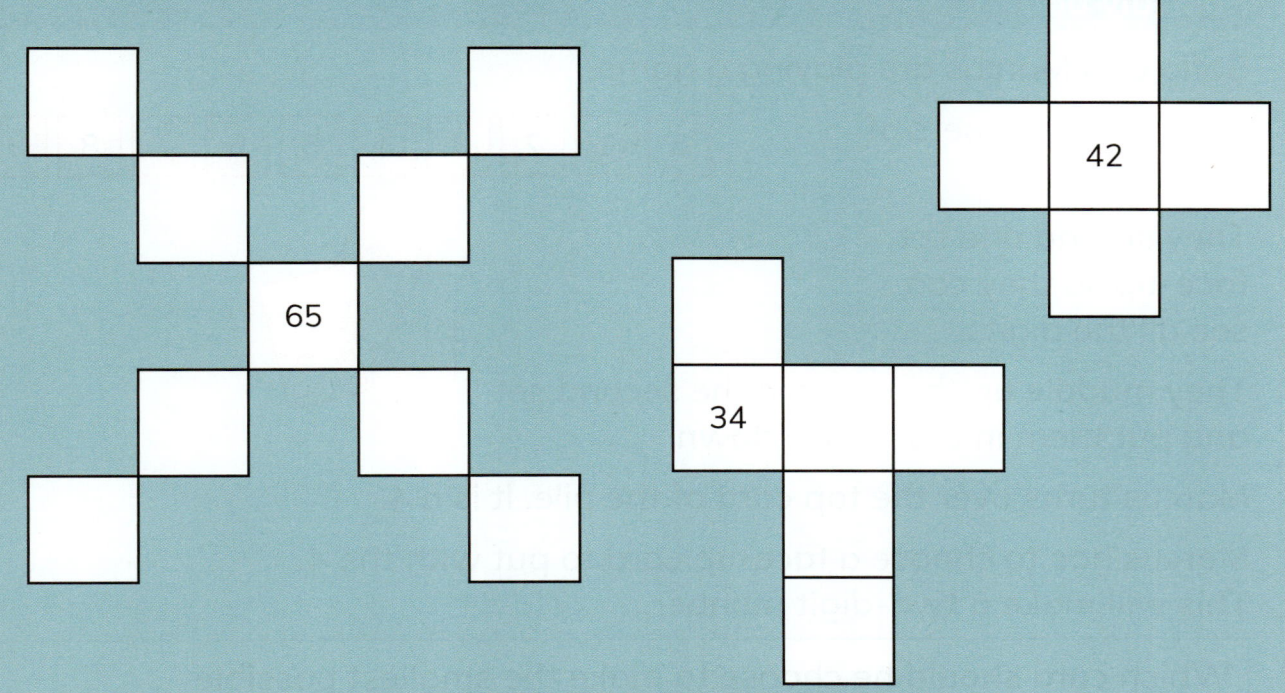

    (piece with 65 in centre)

    (piece with 34)

    (piece with 42)

2. Isaac's number sequence is 69, 67, 65, 63, 61.
   Complete the description of his number sequence.

   _____ at 69. Count _____ in _____ . Stop at _____ .

3. Show 18, 56 and 92 on this number line.

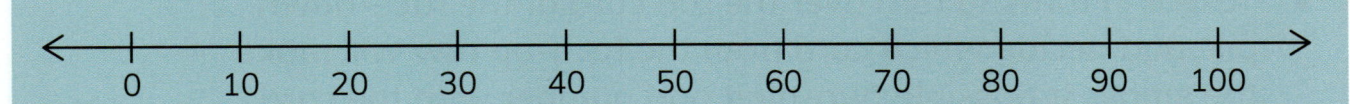

   ←—+—+—+—+—+—+—+—+—+—+—→
   0 10 20 30 40 50 60 70 80 90 100

4. Order these numbers from smallest to greatest.

   | 16 | 67 | 77 | 61 | 76 |

   Use a place value grid or a number line to help you.

Project 1 Possibly odd

Project 1

Possibly odd

Sofia and Marcus are playing a game.

They have two sets of 0–9 digit cards.

| 0 | 1 | 2 | 3 | 4 | 5 | 6 | 7 | 8 | 9 |

They spread one set face-up so they can see all the digits.

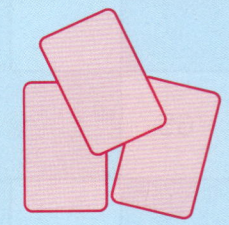

They muddle up the cards in the second set and put them in a pile face down.

Marcus turns over the top card of the pile. It is a 4.

Marcus has to choose a face-up card to put with the 4. This will make a two-digit number.

> Which card should he choose to make the smallest possible odd number? Why?

Try this for yourself with a partner.

- Set out two sets of 0–9 digit cards in the same way that Sofia and Marcus did.
- Take it in turns to turn over the top card of the face-down pile and decide which card from the face-up row will make the smallest possible two-digit odd number with the card you've turned over.

Talk with your partner about a good way of doing this each time. Try it lots of times so that you are sure your way works well. Can you explain your way to someone else? Or write it down?

> How would your way of playing change if you had to make the largest possible odd number?

2 Geometry

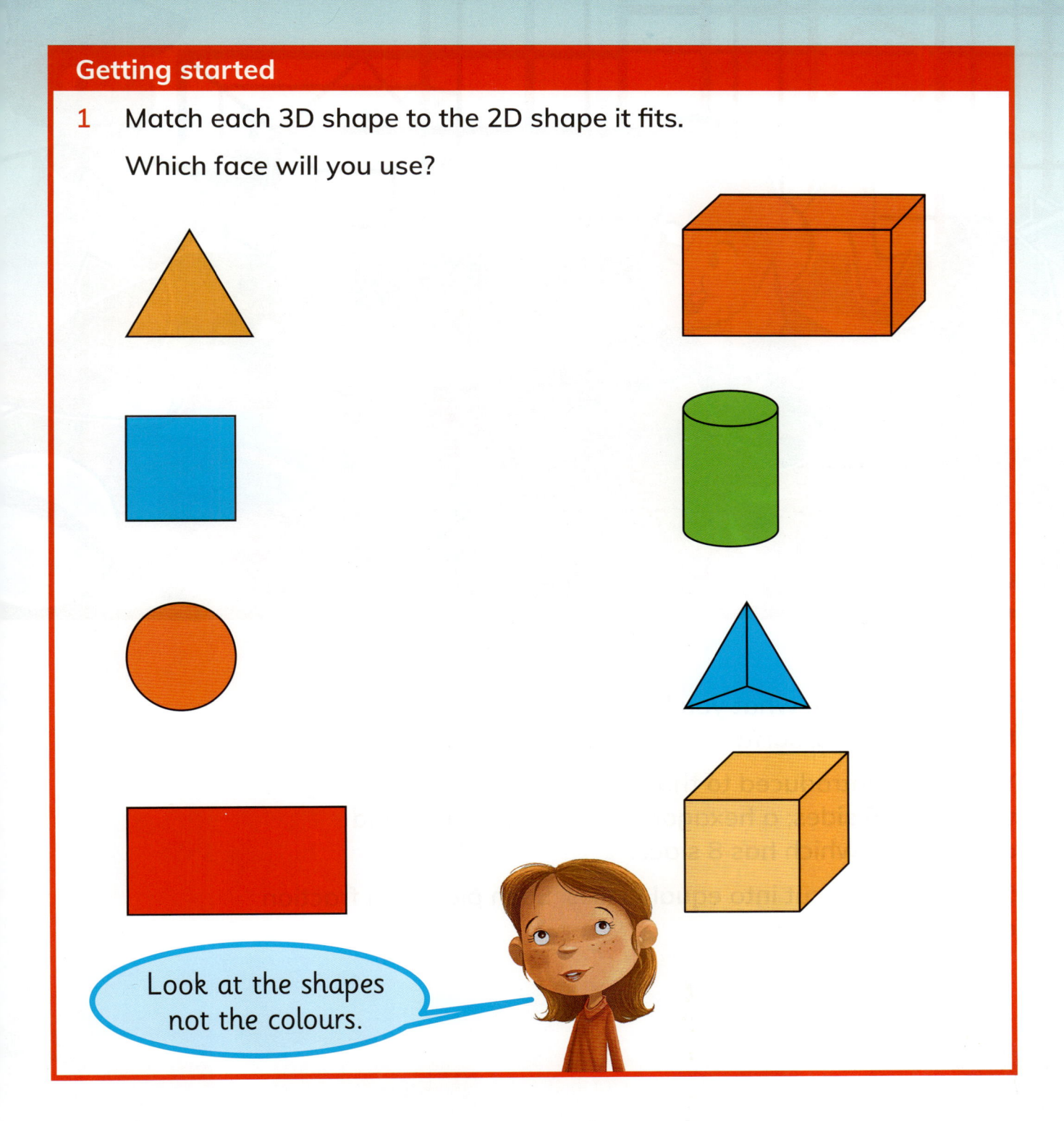

Getting started

1 Match each 3D shape to the 2D shape it fits.

Which face will you use?

Look at the shapes not the colours.

This unit will use what you know about 2D and 3D shapes to explore faces, surfaces, edges and vertices.

You will be introduced to three new 2D shapes: a pentagon, which has 5 sides; a hexagon, which has 6 sides and an octagon, which has 8 sides.

Shapes can be cut into equal pieces. Each piece is a fraction of the whole shape.

> 2.1 3D shapes

> **We are going to ...**
> - identify and describe 3D shapes around us
> - sort and name 3D shapes.

You will see 3D shapes all around you but do you know what they are? This section will help you to recognise 3D shapes in different places. You will also learn more about spheres, cubes, cuboids, pyramids and cylinders.

curved surface   edge
face   vertex, vertices

A vertex is a corner. 'Vertices' is the plural of 'vertex' and means more than one corner.

Exercise 2.1

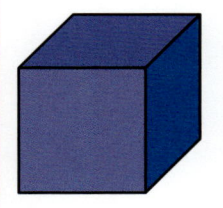

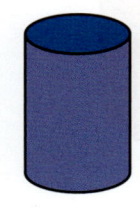

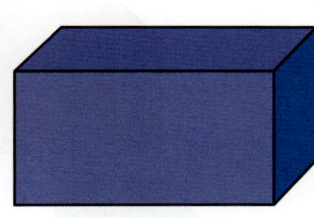

> **Worked example 1**
>
> Imagine painting one face of these shapes.
> Print that face onto paper.
>
> Match each print to the 3D shape that it comes from.
>
> *I think this comes from the cuboid because the 4 sides are not the same length as each other.*
>
> *I think this comes from the cube because it has four straight sides.*
>
> *I think this comes from the cylinder because it's the only shape with no straight lines.*

31

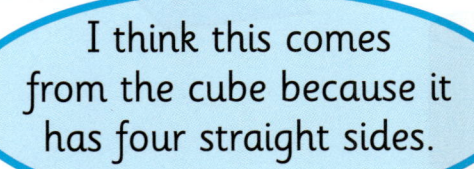

2 Geometry

1 Fill in the missing numbers.

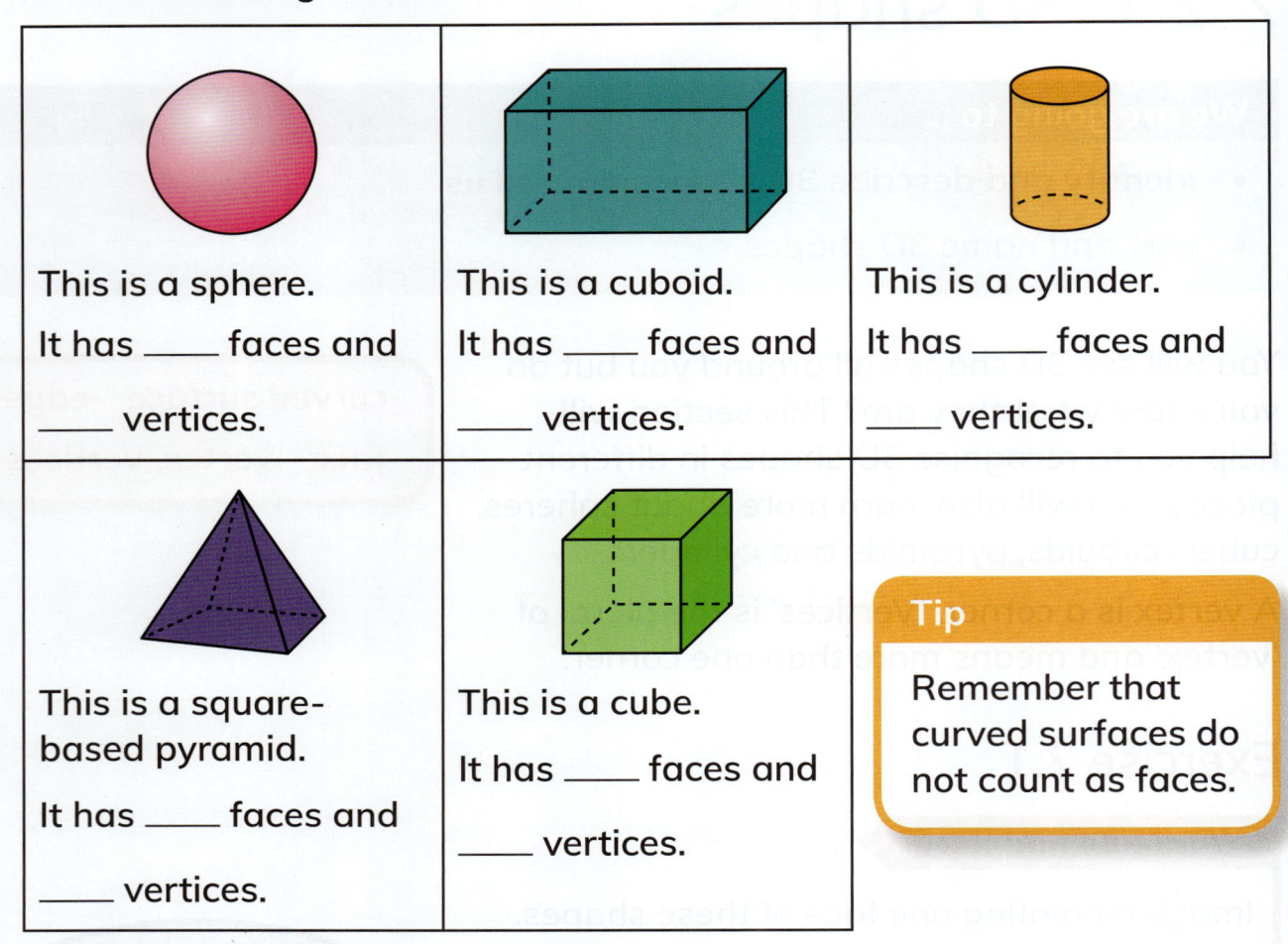

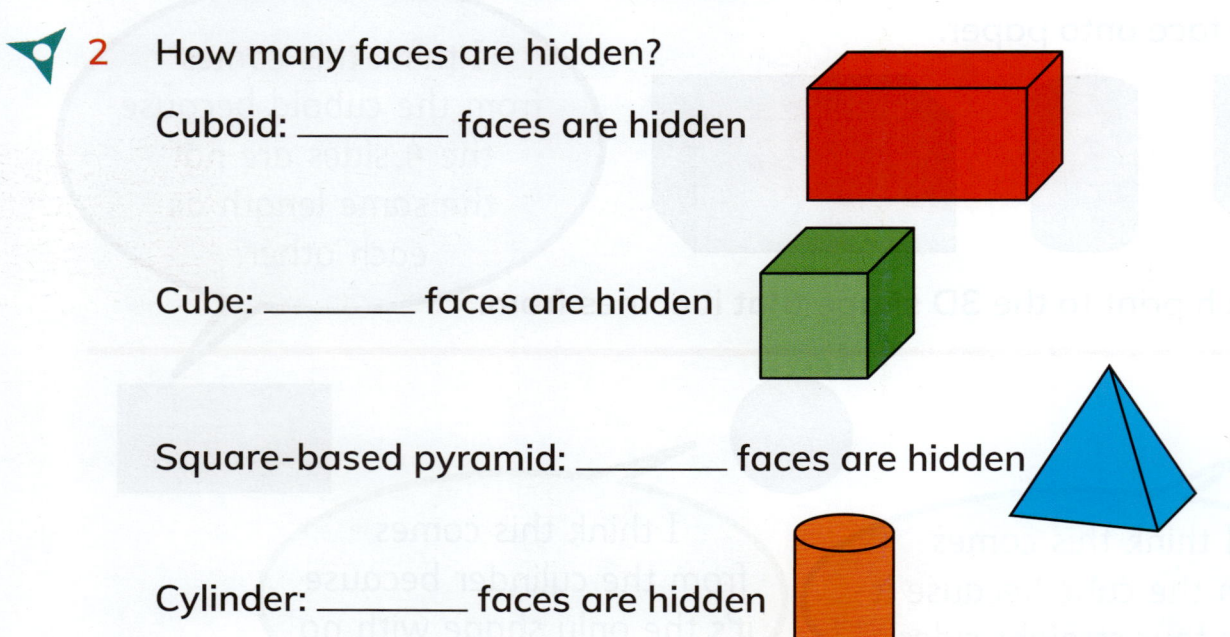

This is a sphere. It has ____ faces and ____ vertices.	This is a cuboid. It has ____ faces and ____ vertices.	This is a cylinder. It has ____ faces and ____ vertices.
This is a square-based pyramid. It has ____ faces and ____ vertices.	This is a cube. It has ____ faces and ____ vertices.	**Tip** Remember that curved surfaces do not count as faces.

2 How many faces are hidden?

Cuboid: _____ faces are hidden

Cube: _____ faces are hidden

Square-based pyramid: _____ faces are hidden

Cylinder: _____ faces are hidden

2.1 3D shapes

3 Draw lines from each shape to sort them according to their properties.

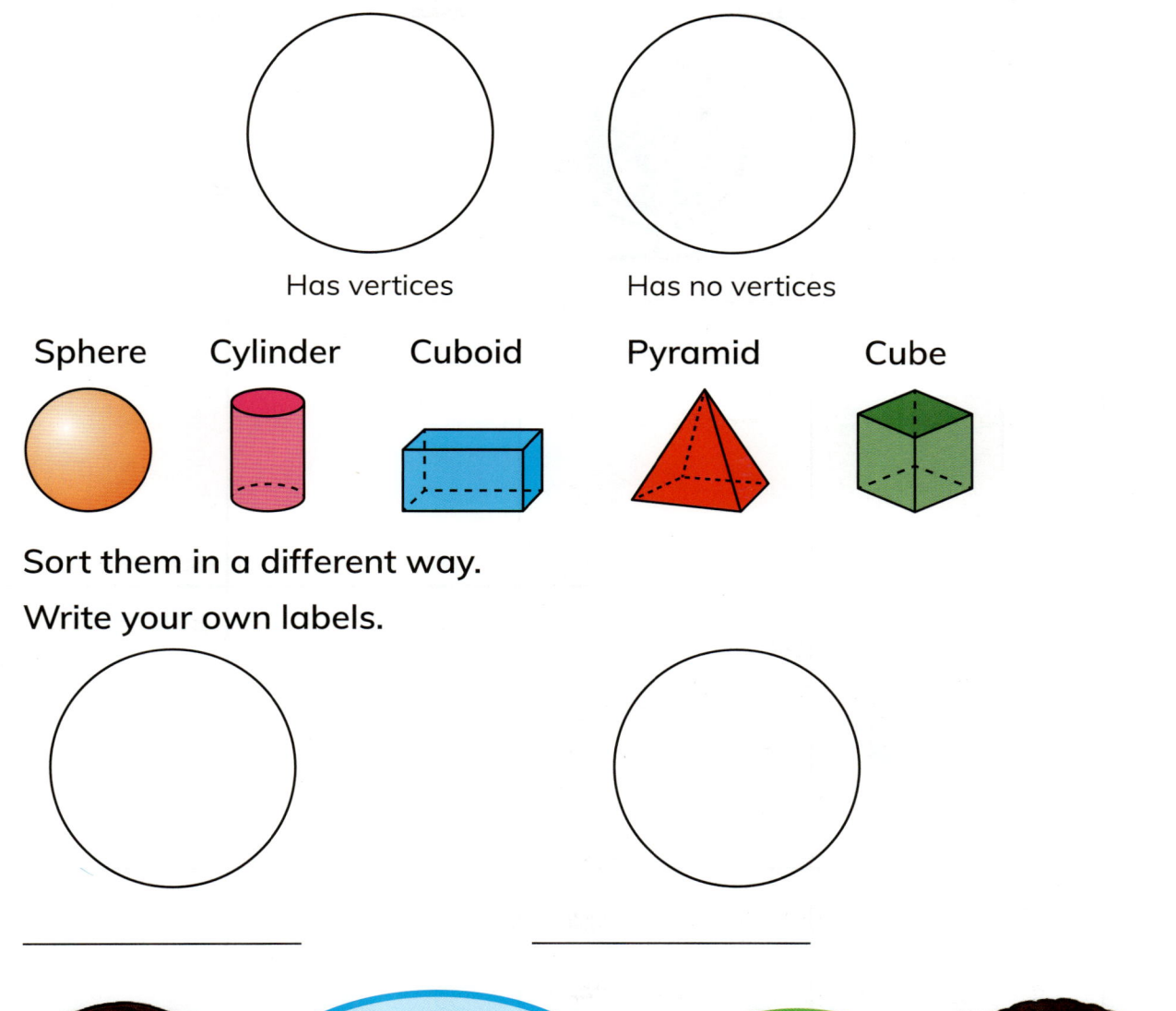

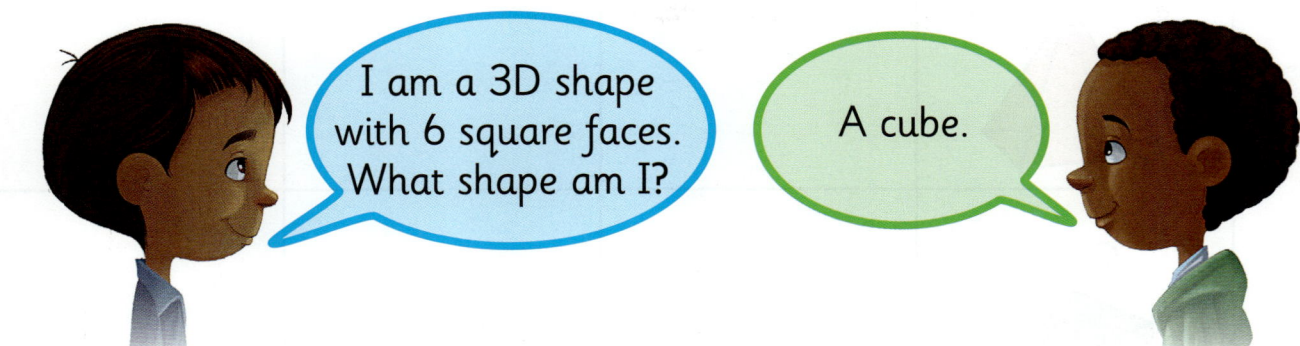

Has vertices   Has no vertices

Sphere   Cylinder   Cuboid   Pyramid   Cube

Sort them in a different way.

Write your own labels.

_____   _____

4

I am a 3D shape with 6 square faces. What shape am I?

A cube.

Play this game with a partner. Take turns to describe the faces of a 3D shape.

Ask your partner to guess what it is.

33

2 Geometry

5 Draw 3 things that match these shapes. The first one is an example.

Sphere	(globe)		
Cylinder			
Cuboid			
Square-based pyramid			
Cube			

34

2.1 3D shapes

Let's investigate

Work with a partner.

Make these shapes using four cubes.

Choose one of the shapes and write how you made it.

_____

_____

_____

_____

Share what you wrote with your partner.

Can they guess what shape you chose?

Did your partner use the correct words to describe the shape? How could they improve their description?

Look what I can do!

- I can identify and describe 3D shapes around me.
- I can sort and name 3D shapes.

35

2 Geometry

> 2.2 2D shape and symmetry

We are going to ...
- learn about symmetry and lines of symmetry
- identify, describe, sort, name and sketch 2D shapes
- identify 2D shapes in familiar objects.

A 2D shape is flat.

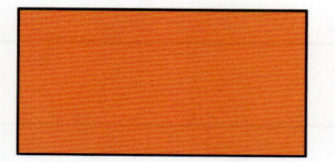

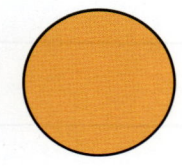

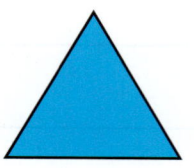

Something is symmetrical when it is **the same on both sides**. A shape has symmetry if a line drawn down (vertical) or across (horizontal) the middle shows that both sides of the shape are exactly the same.

> hexagon   horizontal   line of symmetry   mirror image   octagon
> pentagon   polygon   symmetry   symmetrical   vertical

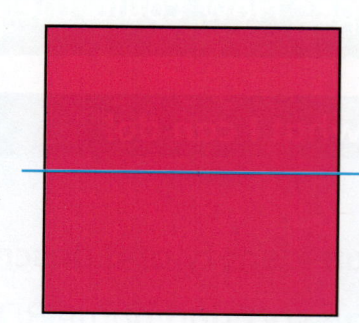

2.2 2D shape and symmetry

Exercise 2.2

Worked example 2

Draw a line of symmetry on this shape.

Answer: This is the vertical line of symmetry.

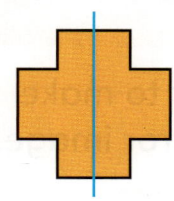

A line of symmetry is a line that you can fold along to make both halves the same.

Answer: This is the horizontal line of symmetry.

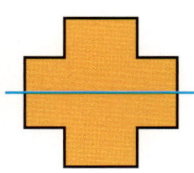

$\frac{1}{2}$ add $\frac{1}{2}$ equals the whole!

1   Find the symmetrical shapes.
    Use a ruler to draw a line of symmetry on them.

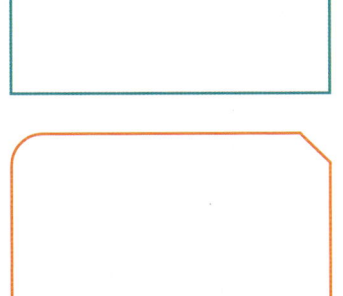

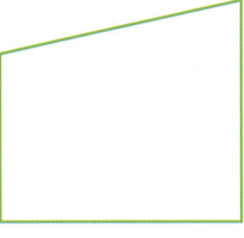

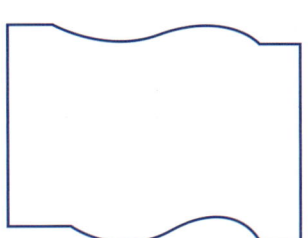

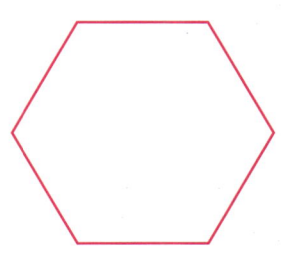

37

2 Geometry

2. Draw a pattern each side of the lines of symmetry to make them symmetrical. The first one is an example.

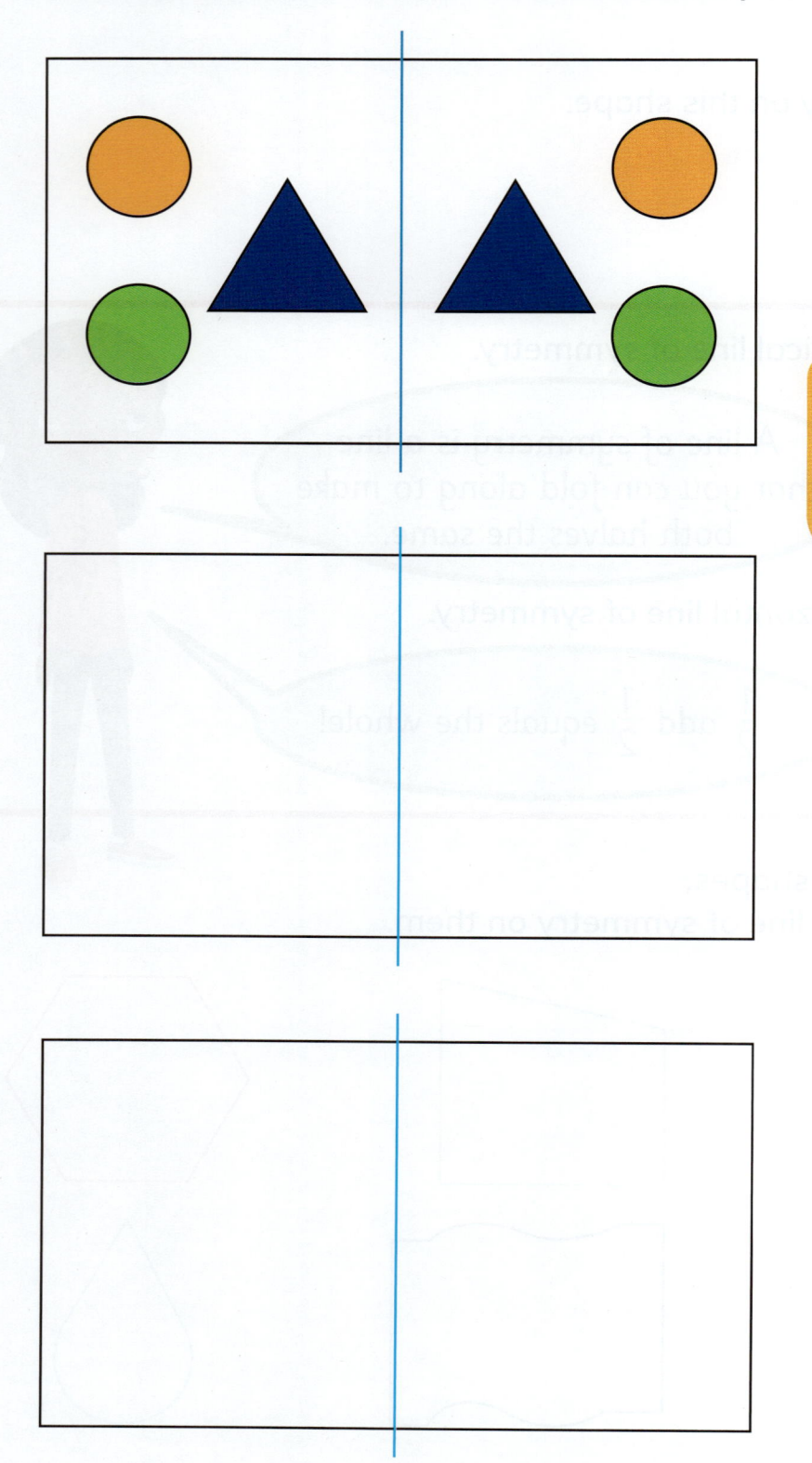

Tip

Remember to make them a mirror image.

38

2.2 2D shape and symmetry

3   Draw the other half of these pictures to make them symmetrical.

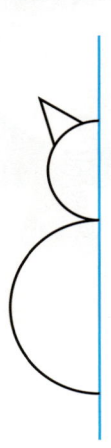

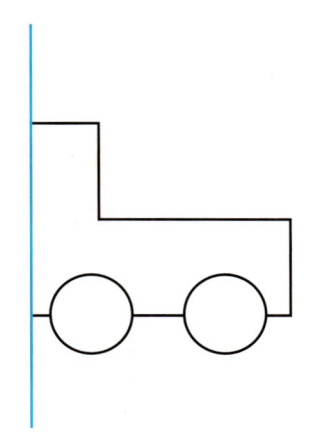

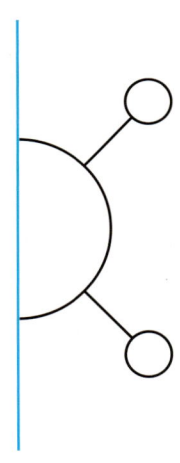

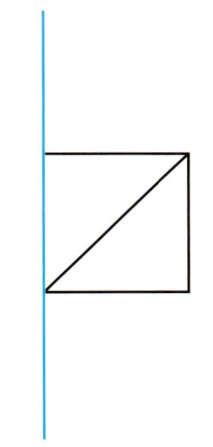

2 Geometry

4 Draw a symmetrical pattern using these shapes. Use 1 line of symmetry. Your pattern can have a vertical or horizontal line of symmetry.

Tip

Remember a line of symmetry is a line that you can fold along to make both halves the same.

2.2 2D shape and symmetry

5   Draw 3 objects that match these shapes. The first one is an example.

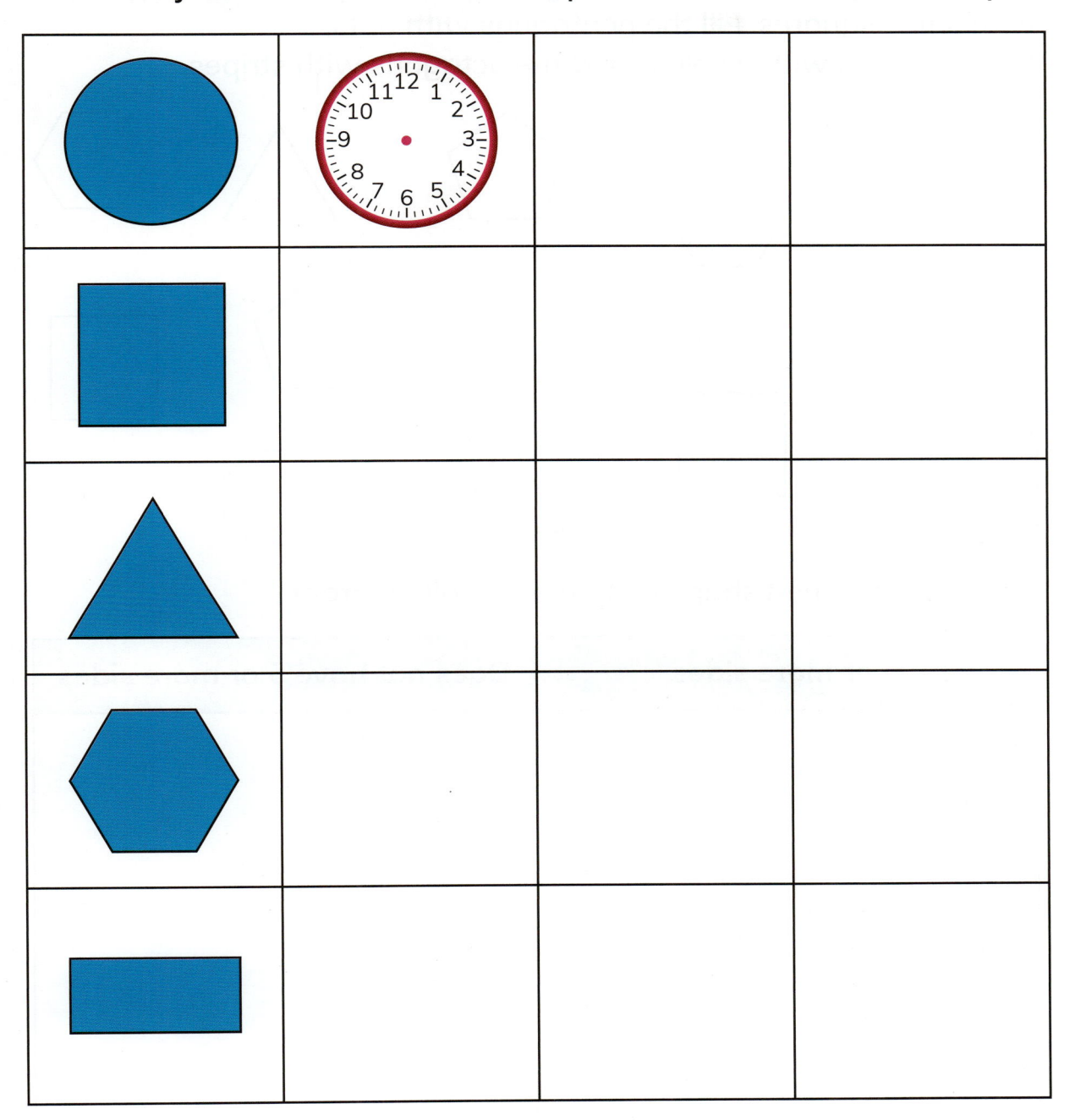

Tip

Look around you. What can you see?

2 Geometry

6   Fill the triangles with small triangles and the squares with small squares. Fill the pentagons with dots, the hexagons with a colour and the octagons with stripes.

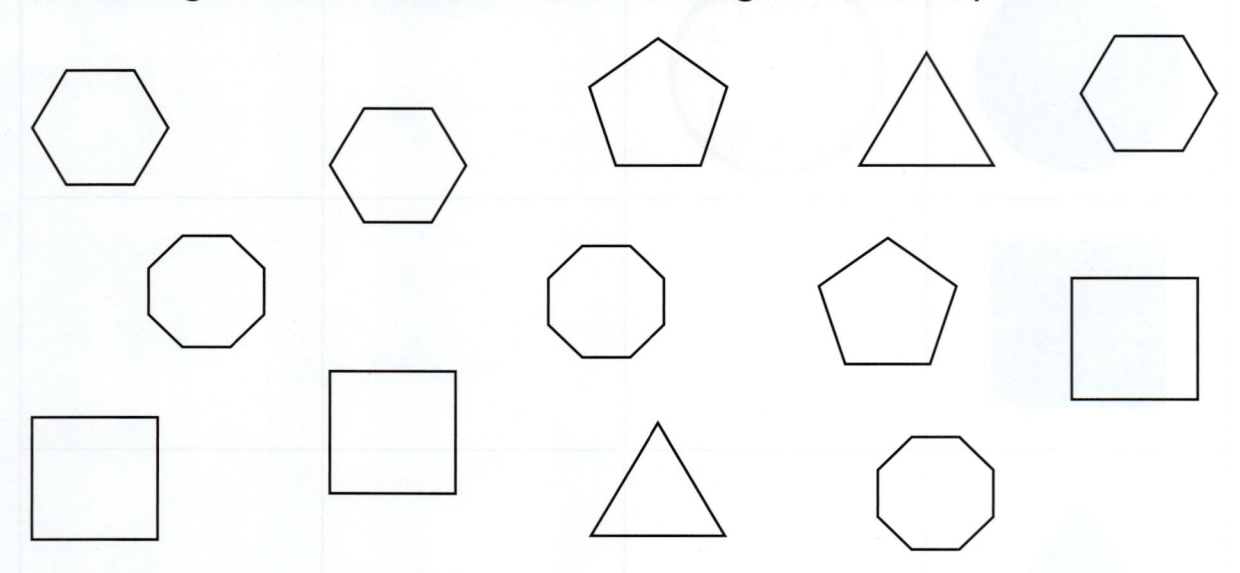

Sort the patterned shapes into the Carroll diagram.

5 or more sides	Does not have 5 or more sides

Draw 2 shapes of your own and put them in the Carroll diagram.

2.2 2D shape and symmetry

7 Colour the rectangles. How many rectangles can you find?

8 How many different ways can you turn the triangle so that it looks different every time?

Draw the shape to show the different ways.

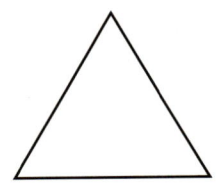

2 Geometry

9 Can you turn a circle so that it looks different?

Explain your answer.

_____

_____

_____

Let's investigate

Work with a partner.

Use up to 10 squares to make different symmetrical shapes.

Always place the shapes edge to edge.

Draw 2 different designs. Use shape and colour to show the symmetry.

What rule are you using when you make symmetrical patterns or pictures?

Can you change the rule?

44

2.2 2D shape and symmetry

10 Colour all the shapes with more than 4 sides.

Circle   Pentagon   Rectangle   Hexagon   Triangle   Octagon

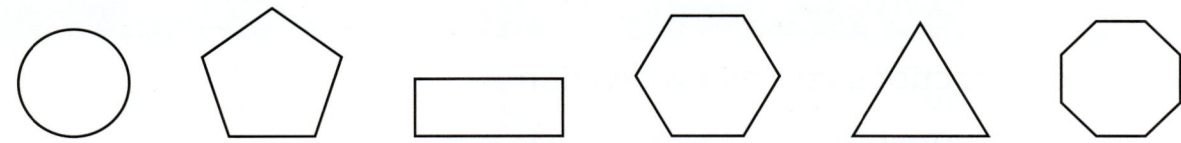

Now sort these shapes. You can draw the shapes or write their names in the sorting circles.

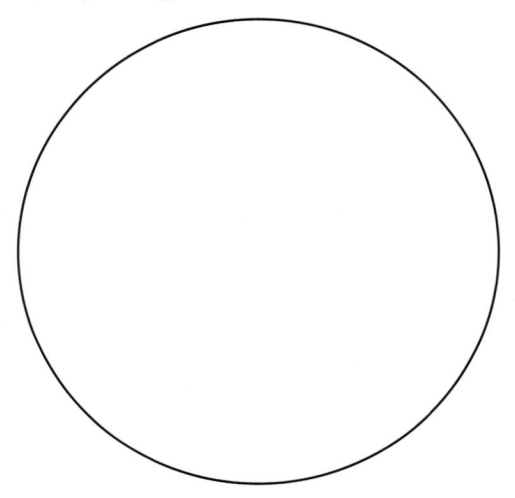

Has 4 vertices or fewer   Has more than 4 vertices

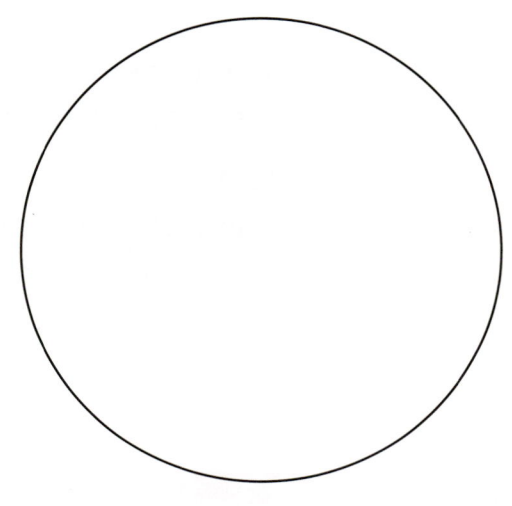

11 Work with a partner and take turns.

Describe a 2D shape. Do not say the name of the shape.

Ask your partner to guess what it is.

Look what I can do!
• I can recognise symmetrical shapes and patterns.
• I can draw symmetrical shapes using a line of symmetry.
• I can identify, describe, sort, name and sketch 2D shapes.
• I can identify 2D shapes in familiar objects.

2 Geometry

2.3 Fractions of shapes

We are going to …
- learn how fractions can mean division
- learn about quarters and three-quarters
- learn how to divide a shape into equal parts.

Fractions are useful in cooking, making and building objects or houses and even sharing a pizza fairly.

Looking at fractions as being equal parts of a whole will help you to understand the difference between equal parts and unequal parts.

equal parts   fraction
quarter   three-quarters

Exercise 2.3

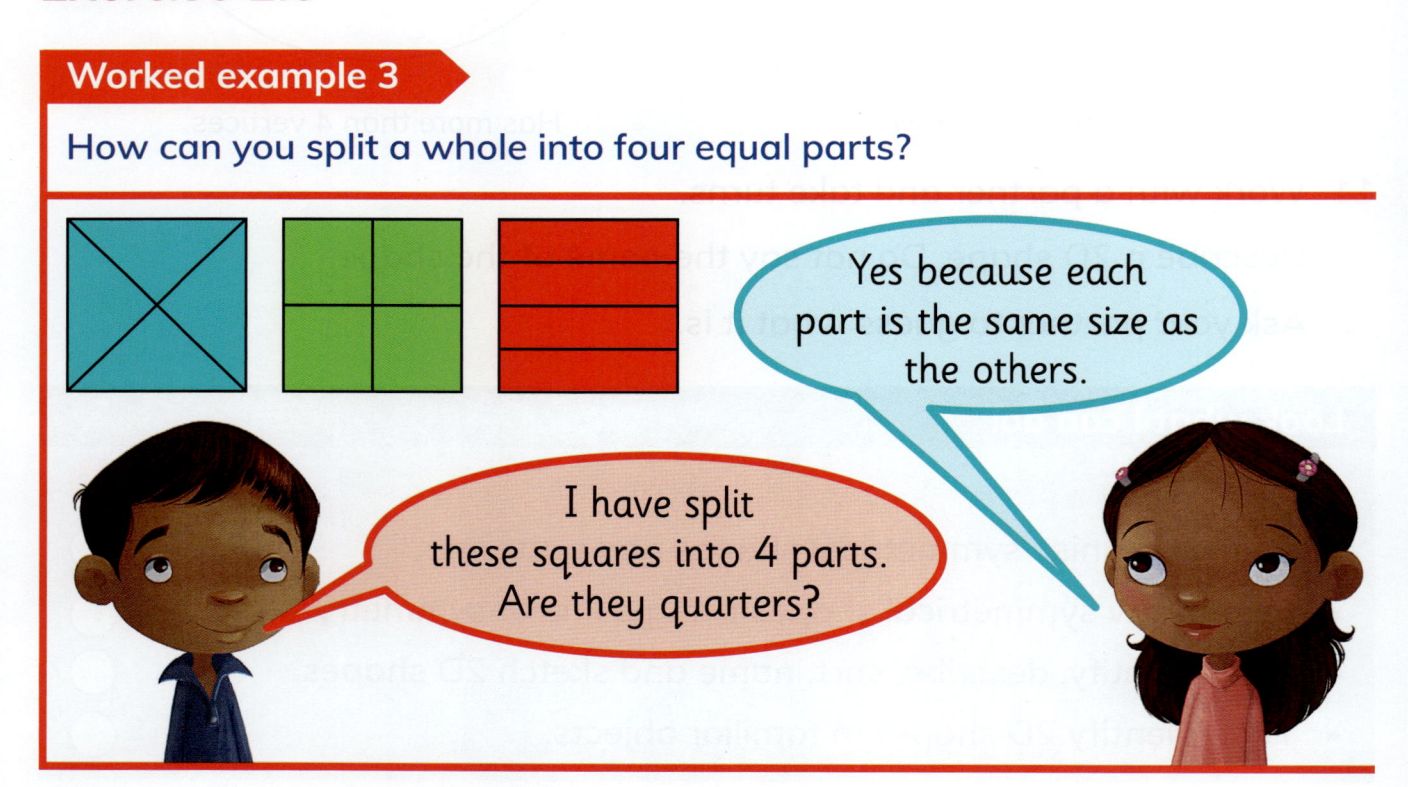

Worked example 3

How can you split a whole into four equal parts?

I have split these squares into 4 parts. Are they quarters?

Yes because each part is the same size as the others.

2.3 Fractions of shapes

1. Here are 4 squares.

   Use a ruler to draw straight lines to show 2 squares divided into halves and 2 squares that are divided into 2 parts but not halves.

   Label the squares $\frac{1}{2}$ or **not** $\frac{1}{2}$.

2. Four boys share a pizza equally.

   How much pizza does each boy have?

   Draw what 1 boy has.

3. Four girls share a pie equally.

   How much pie does each girl have?

   Draw what 2 girls have.

2 Geometry

4 Four children share a large cookie equally.

1 child eats their piece now.

How many quarters are left? _____

5 4 boys share this bar of chocolate equally.

How many squares does each boy have?

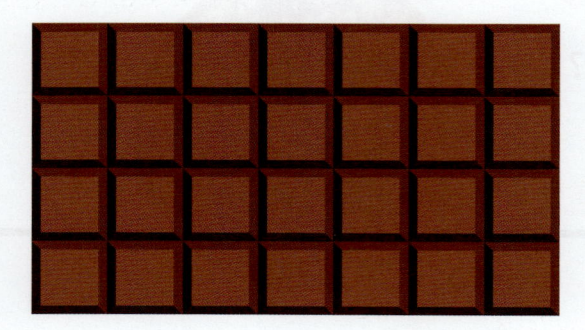

_____

6 a Draw lines to show quarters of these shapes.

Colour one quarter of each shape.

How much of the shape is not coloured? _____

b Draw lines to show quarters of these shapes.

Colour three-quarters of each shape.

How many quarters are not coloured? _____

48

2.3 Fractions of shapes

Let's investigate

Work with a partner.

This is three-quarters of a shape.

What could the whole shape be?

Use blocks or cubes to make your shapes.

Draw your shapes.

Tip

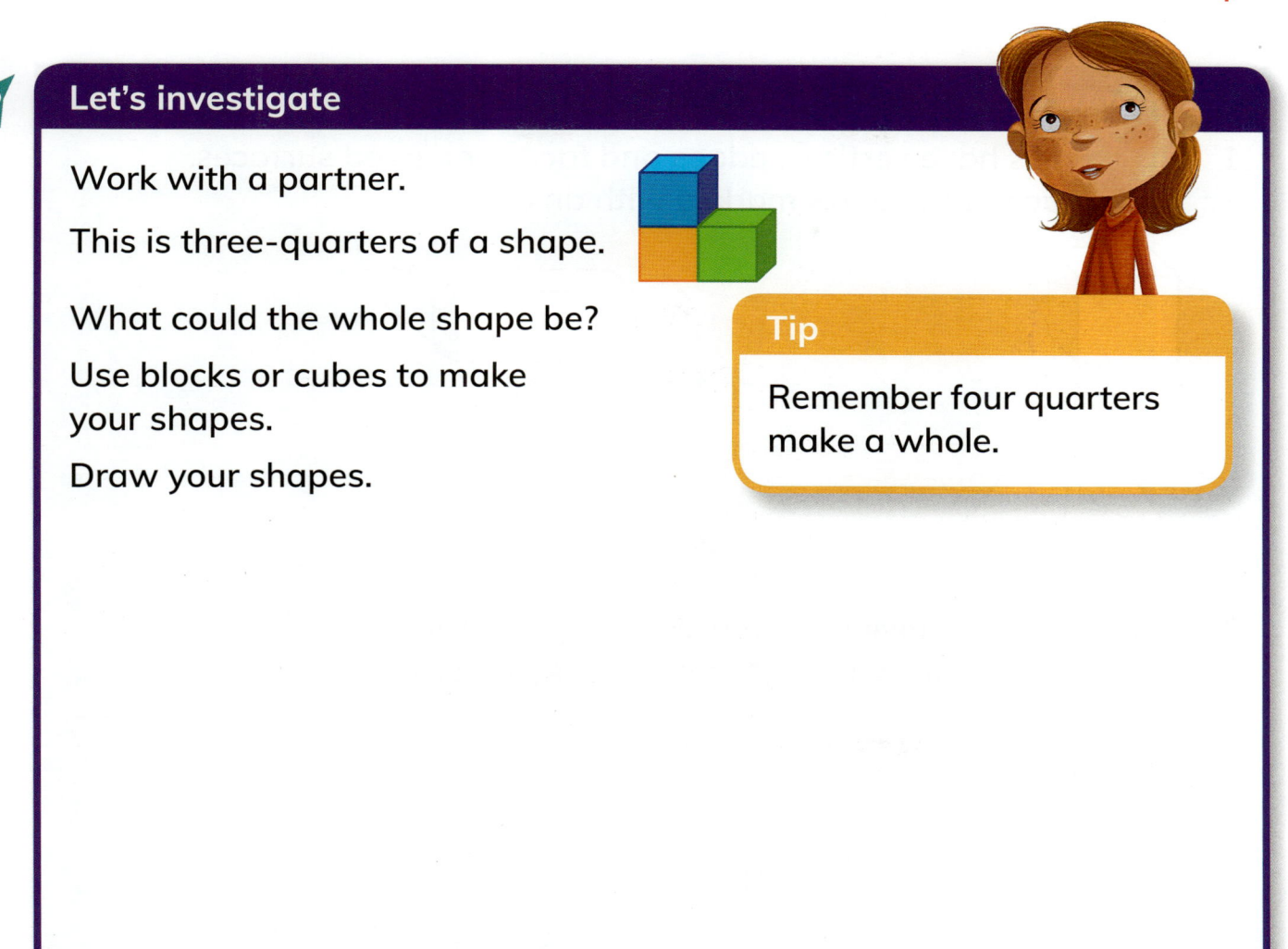

Remember four quarters make a whole.

What is the difference between a half and a quarter?
What happens to the size of the parts when you cut a shape into more parts?

Look what I can do!

- I can recognise quarters and three-quarters of a shape.
- I know how to divide a shape into equal parts.
- I know that fractions can mean division.

2 Geometry

Check your progress

1. 3D shapes have vertices, edges and faces or curved surfaces.
   Label each of the parts marked with an arrow.

2. Which shapes have a vertical line of symmetry?
   Use a ruler to draw the vertical line of symmetry.

3. Write the name of the 2D shapes that are shown in the pictures.

   These shapes are all _____.

Project 2: Strange submarines

> Project 2

Strange submarines

Strange submarines were travelling underwater in the sea. The submarines were all 3D shapes. Some birds flying overhead were looking at the submarines but could only see the outline of each under the water.

Can you say what shapes the submarines might be by looking at their outlines from above?

There may be more than one possibility for each outline.

51

3 Measures

Getting started

1   Draw 2 of your friends.

    Which friend is shorter? _____

    Which friend is taller? _____

3 Measures

WILL IT FIT?

This unit will introduce you to units of measure.

You will practise estimating and measuring the length of lines.

You will draw lines using a ruler.

3 Measures

> 3.1 Length

We are going to ...

- estimate and measure lengths using centimetres and metres
- use a ruler and metre ruler to measure length
- find the difference between two lengths.

In this section you will learn more about length using centimetres and metres. You will use a ruler and a metre ruler. Centimetres are best for shorter lengths and metres for longer ones.

It is important to remember how to use a ruler.

Look at these two rulers.

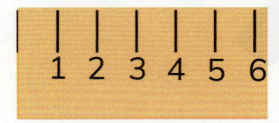

This ruler begins at the edge.
We measure from the edge.

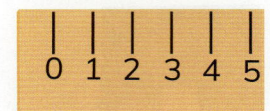

The mark for 0 is not at the edge.
We measure from 0.

Tip

Look at the edge of your ruler. Which type do you have?

Each number on your ruler stands for a centimetre.

A metre is **longer** than a centimetre. A metre is made of 100 centimetres.

The length of an object is the distance from one end of it to the other, along its longest side.

Measuring the shortest side gives us the width of the object. When we measure how tall or high something is, we are finding its height.

centimetre   distance   estimate
height   just over   just under
length   metre   ruler   width

3.1 Length

Exercise 3.1

> **Worked example 1**
>
> How wide is your table?
>
> Estimate first and then measure.

I estimate that the table is 30 hand widths wide. I measured it and it is 26 hand widths wide.

I think it will be about 20 hand widths wide. I measured the table width as about 18 of my hand widths.

Who is right?

We both are. My hand is wider than your hand so I can cover the table using fewer hands.

55

3 Measures

1. Estimate and then measure the length of these pictures. Use a ruler.

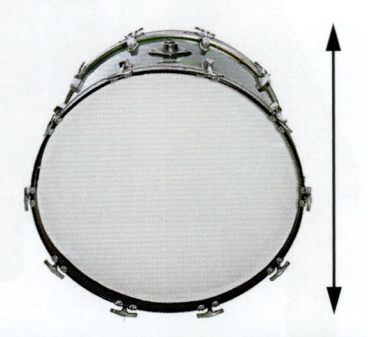

Estimate	Measure

Estimate	Measure

Estimate	Measure

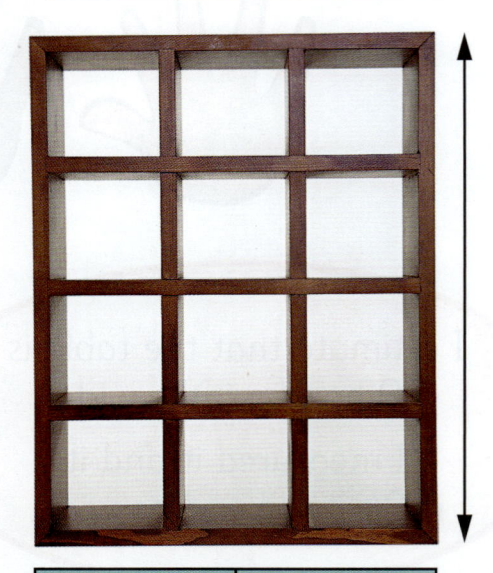

Estimate	Measure

Which is the tallest? _____

Which is the narrowest? _____

56

3.1 Length

2   Work with a partner.

Use a metre ruler to measure your height.

Are you one metre tall, just over one metre tall or just under one metre tall?

Use a metre ruler to measure these lengths.

Estimate first, then measure.

Object	Estimate (centimetres)	Measure (centimetres)
The length of your table		
The height of your table		
The height of a door		
The width of a door		
The distance from your table to the door		
The height of your chair		

3 Measures

3. These ladders can be joined together to make different heights.

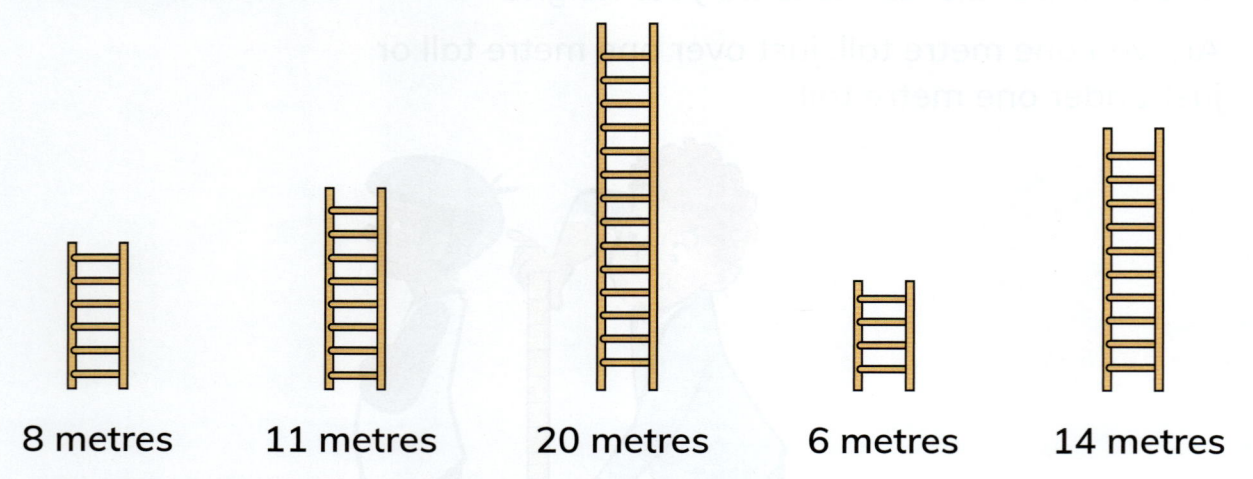

   8 metres   11 metres   20 metres   6 metres   14 metres

   Which ladders are joined together to make exactly these heights?

   a 14 metres _____

   b 26 metres _____

   c 25 metres _____

   d 31 metres _____

   e 20 metres _____

4. This rope is 24 metres long.

   If 14 metres of rope is cut off, how much is left?

   The difference between 24 and 14 is _____

3.1 Length

5. These rulers are in centimetres. Find out the length of each coloured bar using the rulers underneath.

a

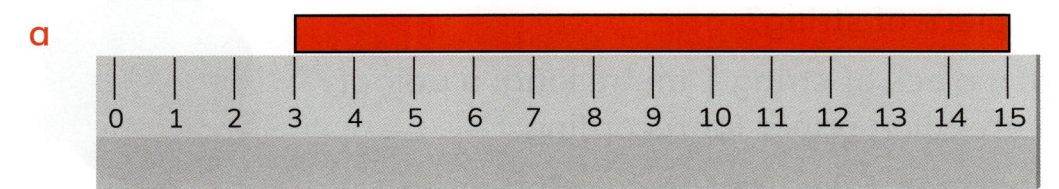

_____ centimetres

b

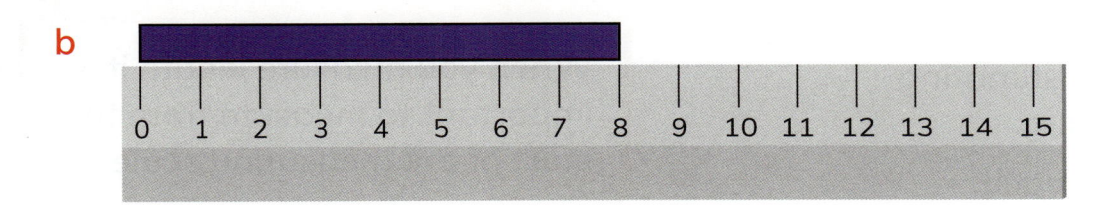

_____ centimetres

c

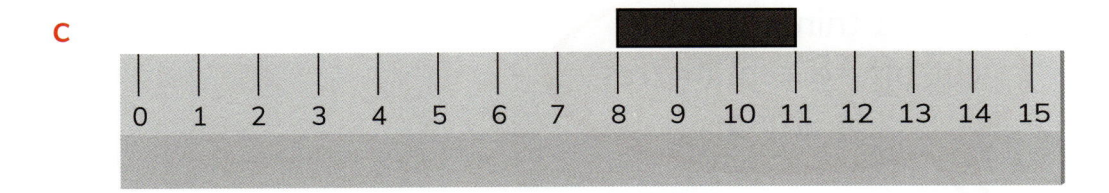

_____ centimetres

d

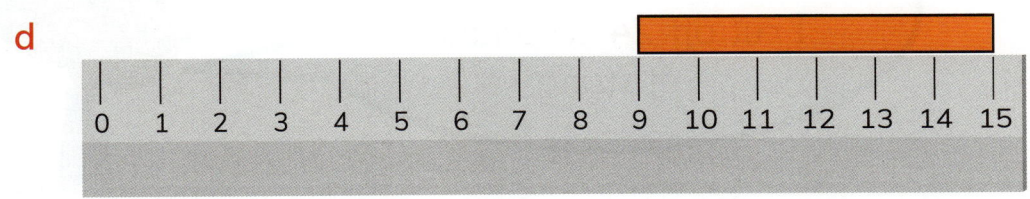

_____ centimetres

Tip

The bars do not all start at 0. Start measuring from where the bars start.

59

3 Measures

Let's investigate

How long is a piece of string?

You will need: a piece of string 1 metre long; a pair of scissors; a metre ruler; paper for recording.

Work with a partner. Take turns to cut off a piece of string.

Estimate the length that you cut off, then measure it.

Repeat the estimating and measuring.

Make 3 cuts each.

Estimate and measure the length of string that is left.

Tip

When you measure length it is important to measure from the start of the measuring scale.

I think you cut off 18 centimetres of string.

I think I cut off more than that. I think I cut off 24 centimetres of string.

Is it possible to end up with the same length left if we did more or fewer cuts?

3.2 Drawing and measuring lines

Look what I can do!	😐	🙂
• I can estimate and measure lengths using centimetres and metres.	○	○
• I can find the difference between two lengths.	○	○
• I can use a ruler and metre ruler to measure length.	○	○

> 3.2 Drawing and measuring lines

We are going to …

- draw and measure lines using centimetres
- use a ruler and a metre ruler as a number line.

In this section you will use what you know about measuring with centimetres. It is important to remember how to use your ruler when drawing and measuring.

Exercise 3.2

1 Which line is longer?

I think the _____ line is longer.

Which line is shorter?

I think the _____ line is shorter.

61

3 Measures

2. You will make strips of paper of different lengths and widths. You will need an A4 piece of paper. Use your ruler and draw a line 5 centimetres below the longest edge of your paper (see the bottom line in strip 1 in the picture below).

    Measure the length of this line and draw the next strip 5 centimetres shorter and 1 centimetre narrower.

    Keep measuring 5 centimetres shorter and 1 centimetre narrower for each new strip, until you have drawn 4 strips.

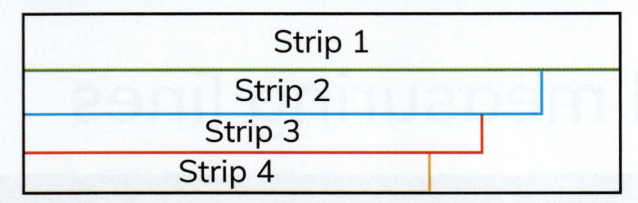

    Strip 1
    Strip 2
    Strip 3
    Strip 4

    Cut along the lines you have drawn.
    You now have 4 strips of paper.

    Bend them round and stick the edges together.

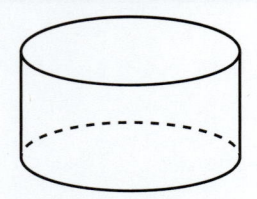

    You now have 4 rings.

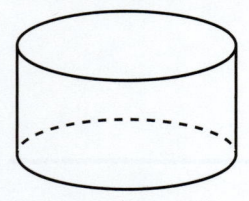

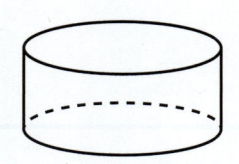

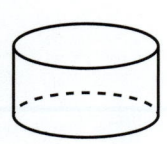

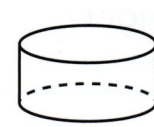

    Can they fit inside each other?
    Now you are ready to decorate them.

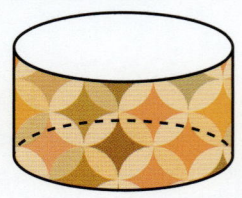

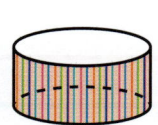

3.2 Drawing and measuring lines

3   Let's make a ruler!

Make a rod of 15 or more centimetre cubes.

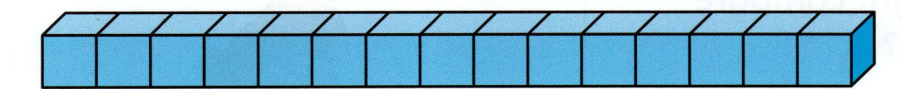

Cut a strip of paper.

Lay the cubes on top of your paper.

Make sure you put the edge of a cube at the left edge of the paper.

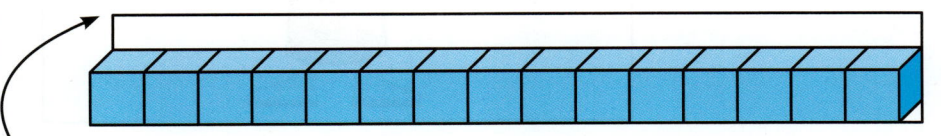

This left edge will be 0. (There is no space to write 0 on your ruler.)

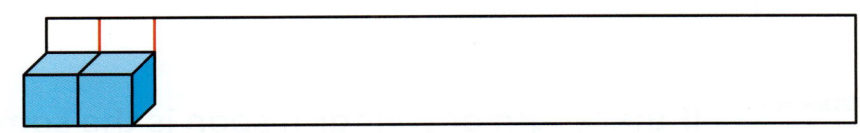

Where 2 cubes meet, draw a line on your paper.

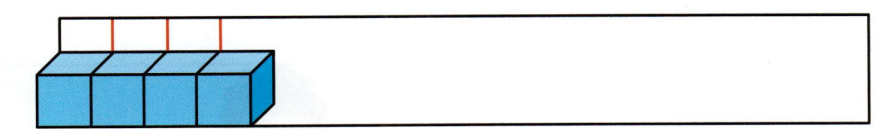

Keep on adding cubes. Keep on drawing lines until you reach the end of your paper.

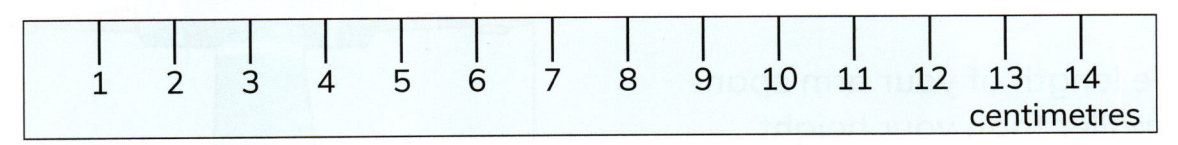

Write numbers on your ruler. Write 'centimetres' on your ruler.

Use your ruler to measure lots of different things at home and at school.

3 Measures

Let's investigate

How does your height compare with your arm span?

If the length of your arm span is larger than your height, you are a wide rectangle.

If the length of your arm span is the same as your height, you are a square.

If the length of your arm span is smaller than your height, you are a tall rectangle.

3.2 Drawing and measuring lines

> **Continued**
>
> Draw a picture of yourself. What shape are you?
>
> I am _____

Do you think that everyone in the class is the same shape as you? How could you find out?

Look what I can do

- I can draw and measure lines using centimetres.
- I can use a ruler and a metre ruler as a number line.

3 Measures

Check your progress

1. Estimate and measure the lengths of these lines.

Estimate	Measure

Estimate	Measure

2. Draw 2 things that you would measure using a metre ruler.
Draw one of them to show height.
Draw one of them to show length.

3.2 Drawing and measuring lines

Continued

3   Measure the length of these rectangles using centimetres.

Draw a shorter line than the shortest rectangle.
Draw a longer line than the longest rectangle.
Measure and write their lengths.

4 Statistics

Getting started

1. Draw lines to sort the animals into the correct boxes in the Carroll diagram.

Spots	Not spots

68

4 Statistics

Continued

2   2 animals are in the wrong place in the Carroll diagram.

Draw a ring around them.

4 legs	Not 4 legs

Draw an animal of your own in each section.

This unit will show you two different ways to sort and show data you have collected.

You will use what you know about Carroll diagrams and learn about tally charts.

4 Statistics

> 4.1 Carroll diagrams and tally charts

We are going to ...
- conduct an investigation to answer non-statistical and statistical questions
- record, organise and represent data using a tally chart and a Carroll diagram
- describe data and discuss conclusions.

A Carroll diagram is used to sort objects according to whether they have or have not a given feature, for example, if a set of animals have legs or not.

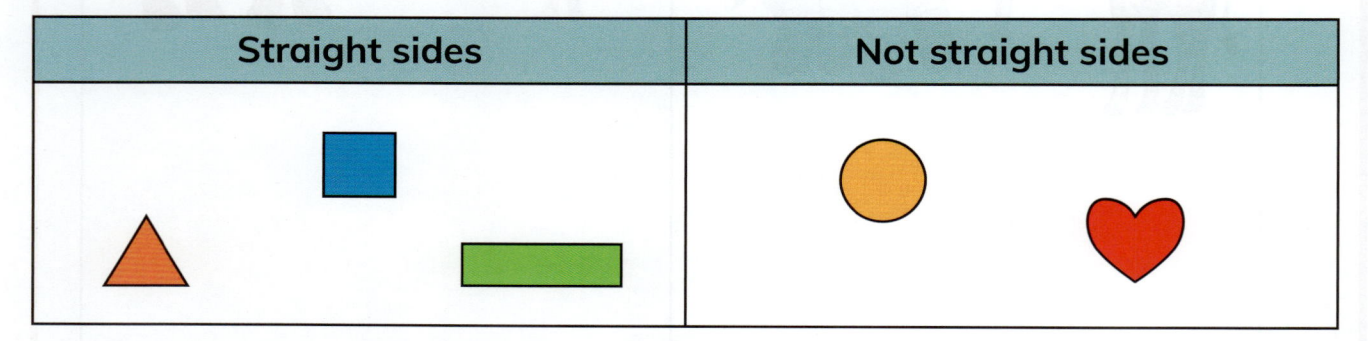

Straight sides	Not straight sides
■ ▲ ▬	● ♥

You can sort for two different things at the same time on this Carroll diagram.

	Triangles	Not triangles
Spotty	△ ▽	● ♥
Not spotty	▲ ▲ ▲	■ ▬

70

4.1 Carroll diagrams and tally charts

A tally chart uses marks known as a tally.
The marks are grouped in fives.

1	I	6	⊮ I
2	II	7	⊮ II
3	III	8	⊮ III
4	IIII	9	⊮ IIII
5	⊮	10	⊮ ⊮

Carroll diagram
least popular   most popular
non-statistical question
statistical question
tally   tally chart

Tally charts are used to collect data quickly. One mark shows one object. When you get to five lines, the fifth line is crossed through the first four. This makes counting at the end easier, as you can count in fives.

Exercise 4.1

1 Use tally marks to record how many vehicles there are in this picture.

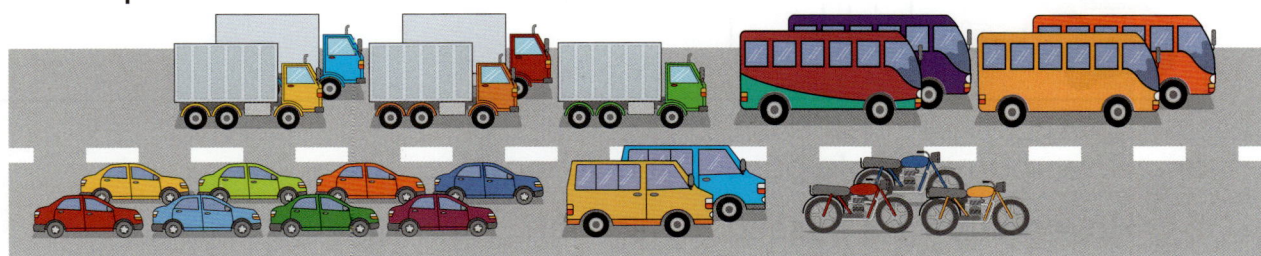

Vehicle	Tally
Cars	
Trucks	
Vans	
Buses	
Bikes	

How many vehicles are there altogether?
Show it using tally marks.

4 Statistics

2 A class made a tally chart of the vehicles and people they saw passing the school in the morning.

Things that pass the school	
Thing	**Tally**
person	‖‖‖ ‖‖‖ ‖‖‖ ‖
car	‖‖‖ ‖‖‖ ‖‖‖ ‖‖‖ ‖‖‖ ‖‖‖ ‖‖‖‖
bus	‖‖‖ ‖‖‖
motorcycle	‖‖
truck	‖‖‖ ‖

a How many **people** passed the school? _____

b How many **cars** passed the school? _____

c How many **vehicles** passed the school? _____
   Show the total number of vehicles that passed as tally marks.

d What if there are double the number of buses and cars? Calculate the total of them. Show it as tally marks.

4.1 Carroll diagrams and tally charts

3 The teacher of a class looked at the snacks her learners brought to school.

She made a tally chart of what she saw.

Use the tally chart to answer these questions.

Snack tally chart	
Snack	Tally
fruit	|||| |||| ||||
cake	||||	
crisps	||||
chocolate	|||| |||

a How many had fruit? _____
b How many had cake? _____
c How many had crisps? _____
d How many had chocolate? _____
e Which snack is most common? _____
f Which snack is the least common? _____
g How many fewer learners have crisps than fruit? _____
h How many more learners have chocolate than cake? _____

4 Here is a Carroll diagram.

Write the numbers in their correct places on the diagram.

More than 10	Not more than 10

14   3   18   7   2   5   13   20   17   8
4   19   6   11   1   15   12   9   16

4 Statistics

5   Choose ten 2-digit numbers less than 50.
    Write them in the boxes.

    Sort your numbers into the Carroll diagram.

	More than 20	Not more than 20
Even		
Not even		

6   Arun did a survey to see how many of his friends could swim and ride a bike. He showed the results in a Carroll diagram.

	Can ride a bike	Cannot ride a bike
Can swim	𝍳𝍳𝍳𝍳𝍳 ǀǀ	ǀǀǀǀ
Cannot swim	𝍳𝍳𝍳𝍳𝍳 ǀ	𝍳𝍳𝍳𝍳𝍳

    Use the diagram to answer these questions.

    a   ____ children can swim.

    b   ____ children cannot ride a bike.

    c   ____ children cannot swim and cannot ride a bike.

    d   ____ children can swim and can ride a bike.

4.1 Carroll diagrams and tally charts

7   What is your favourite colour?
    Ask 10 learners in your class.
    On a piece of paper, draw a tally chart to show the results.

    Write 4 things that the tally chart shows you.

    1 _____

    2 _____

    3 _____

    4 _____

8   Ask 10 learners in your class how they get to and from school.

    How will you record the answers? _____

    Explain why you chose that way.

    _____

    Find and write 4 things that your data shows you.

    1 _____

    2 _____

    3 _____

    4 _____

    Share your results with a partner. Are they the same or different?

    Write what is the same and what is different.

    _____

    _____

75

4 Statistics

> **Let's investigate**
>
> Work with a partner.
>
> Make a tally chart to record how many times each number on a dice lands.
>
> Throw a dice 10 times and record the numbers you throw.
>
> | Number | Tally |
> |--------|-------|
> | 1 | |
> | 2 | |
> | 3 | |
> | 4 | |
> | 5 | |
> | 6 | |
>
> _____ was thrown the most.
> It was thrown _____ times.
>
> Do you think that number will show the most if you throw the dice 20 times?
>
> Complete another tally chart and find out.
>
> | Number | Tally |
> |--------|-------|
> | 1 | |
> | 2 | |
> | 3 | |
> | 4 | |
> | 5 | |
> | 6 | |
>
> _____ was shown the most.
> It was shown _____ times.
> _____ was shown the least.
> It was shown _____ times.
>
> What differences are there between the two tables?
> Discuss with your partner.

4.1 Carroll diagrams and tally charts

> What would happen if the dice was thrown 100 times?
> Would the same results show every time?

9   Work as a group of 3 or 4.

   Collect the data you will need to plan a party for the class.

   What questions will you ask your classmates? Each person in your group can ask a different question. Write your question here.

   _____

   _____

   How will you record your data? _____

   Record your data on a piece of paper.

   Write 3 or 4 things your group found out.

   _____

   _____

   _____

Look what I can do!

- I can conduct an investigation to answer non-statistical and statistical questions.
- I can record, organise and represent data using a tally chart and a Carroll diagram.
- I can describe data and discuss conclusions.

77

4 Statistics

Check your progress

1 Use this Carroll diagram to complete the tally chart about girls and boys that own or do not own a cat.

	Own a cat	Do not own a cat
Girls	8	3
Boys	5	7

Person	Tally
Girls who own a cat	
Girls who do not own a cat	
Boys who own a cat	
Boys who do not own a cat	

How many children have cats? _____

How many children have no cats? _____

How many children are there altogether? _____

2 Write the labels for this Carroll diagram.

	1 3 5 7 9	2 4 6 8
	11 13 15 17 19	10 12 14 16 18

5 Working with numbers to 100

Getting started

1. Write all the number bonds for 10.

2. Add 8 and 7. Write your number sentence.

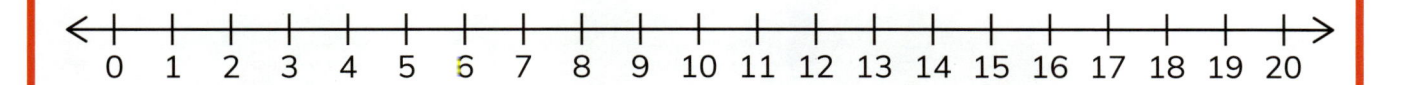

←—+—→
 0 1 2 3 4 5 6 7 8 9 10 11 12 13 14 15 16 17 18 19 20

3. Subtract 5 from 14. Write your number sentence.

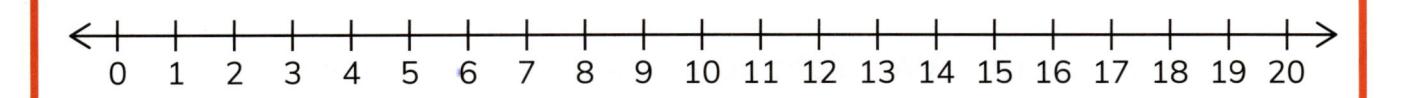

←—+—→
 0 1 2 3 4 5 6 7 8 9 10 11 12 13 14 15 16 17 18 19 20

5 Working with numbers to 100

We calculate every day. We might add to find out how many of something and subtract to find out how many are left.

We can multiply to find out how many there are when we have more than one group the same size.

We can divide to find how many groups we can make.

> 5.1 Addition

> **We are going to ...**
> - add ones or tens to a 2-digit number
> - add 3 or more small numbers together
> - use complements of 10 to find complements of 20 and tens numbers to 100.

You will often need to add two amounts together to find out how many altogether.

As the numbers get larger, counting takes too long and it is easy to make a mistake. A place value grid will help you to calculate.

> column addition
> complement (of 10, 20 and tens numbers to 100)
> place value grid

Exercise 5.1

1   Draw two different arrangements for 7 on the ten frames.

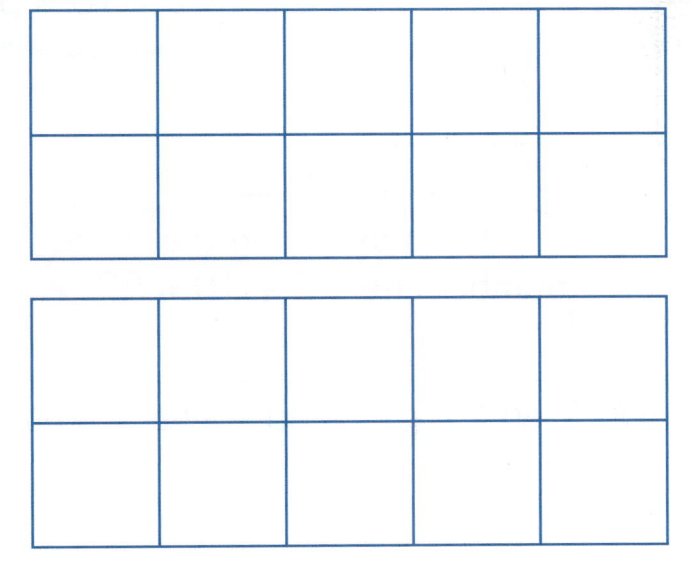

81

5 Working with numbers to 100

2 Find the totals.

a 41 + 6 = ☐   b 35 + 4 = ☐   c 73 + 4 = ☐

d 62 + 7 = ☐   e 37 + 2 = ☐   f 53 + 3 = ☐

3 Find the totals.

a   64   b   71   c   46
   + 5   + 6   + 2

Worked example 1

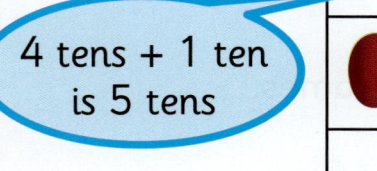

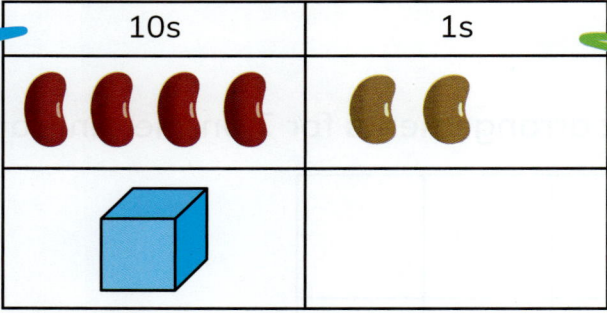

42 + 10 = ☐

10s	1s

4 tens + 1 ten is 5 tens

The ones have not changed. 42 + 10 = 52

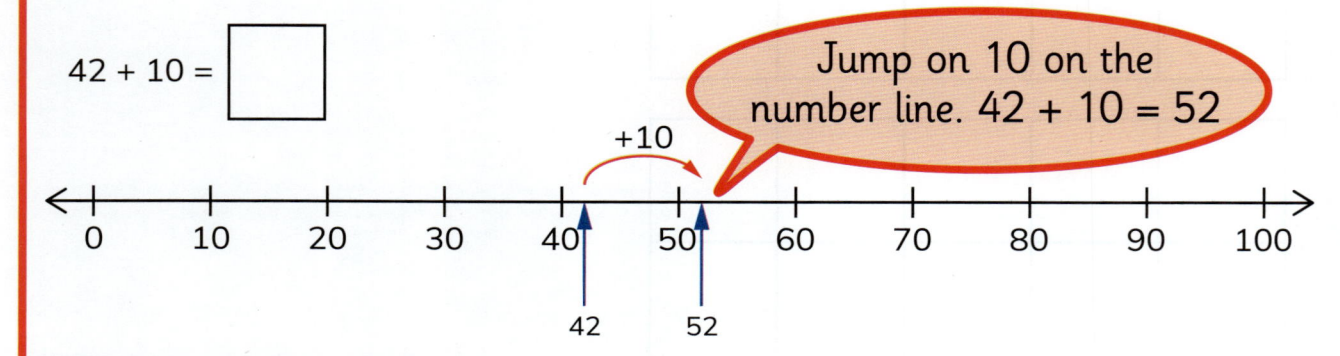

42 + 10 = ☐

Jump on 10 on the number line. 42 + 10 = 52

+10 from 42 to 52 on number line (0 to 100)

Answer: 42 + 10 = 52

5.1 Addition

4 Find the totals.

   a 57 + 10 = ☐   b 34 + 10 = ☐   c 79 + 10 = ☐

   d 48 + 20 = ☐   e 65 + 20 = ☐   f 26 + 30 = ☐

5 Find the totals.

   a   37   b   61   c   56
      + 10   + 20   + 30

> Is it easier to find the total when the calculation is written across the page or down the page?
> Why do you think that might be?
> Share your ideas with your partner.

6 6 + 4 = 10. Use this to help you write two number sentences to show complements of 20 and one number sentence to show complements of 100 using tens numbers.

7 Use the number bonds for 5 to help you write number sentences to show the complements of 50 using tens numbers.

83

5 Working with numbers to 100

> **Worked example 2**
>
> Find the total of these three numbers.
>
> 4 + 5 + 6

4 + 5 + 6 = ☐

4 + 6   = 10

10 + 5 = 15

Answer: 4 + 5 + 6 = 15

> 4 and 6 equal 10. And 5 more is 15.

8   Find the totals.

   a   9 + 6 + 1 = ☐   b   5 + 7 + 5 = ☐   c   7 + 4 + 3 = ☐

Write some calculations that add 4 single-digit numbers for your partner to solve. Swap calculations.

What made the calculations hard or easy? Discuss with your partner.

Let's investigate

Keep adding three single-digit numbers in the same pattern.

1 + 2 + 3 = 6   2 + 3 + 4 = ☐   3 + 4 + 5 = ☐ ...

What do you notice?

Can you say why? Discuss with your partner or in a small group.

> **Look what I can do!**
>
> - I can use complements of 10 to find complements of 20 and tens numbers to 100.
> - I can add ones or tens to a 2-digit number.
> - I can add 3 or more small numbers together.

> 5.2 Subtraction

> **We are going to ...**
>
> - subtract ones from a 2-digit number
> - subtract tens from a 2-digit number
> - identify whether to add or subtract to solve a word problem.

You will often need to subtract one amount from another to find out how many are left.

As the numbers get larger, counting takes too long and it is easy to make a mistake. A place value grid will help you to calculate.

> column subtraction
> operation

Exercise 5.2

1   Find the missing numbers.

a   37 − 5 =

b   46 − 4 =

c   79 − 6 =

d   68 − 7 =

e   59 − 8 =

f   87 − 5 =

5 Working with numbers to 100

2   Find the missing numbers.

a   69
    − 5
    ___

b   49
    − 6
    ___

c   78
    − 7
    ___

> Did you know some of the answers without working them out? Which number bonds did you use?

Worked example 3

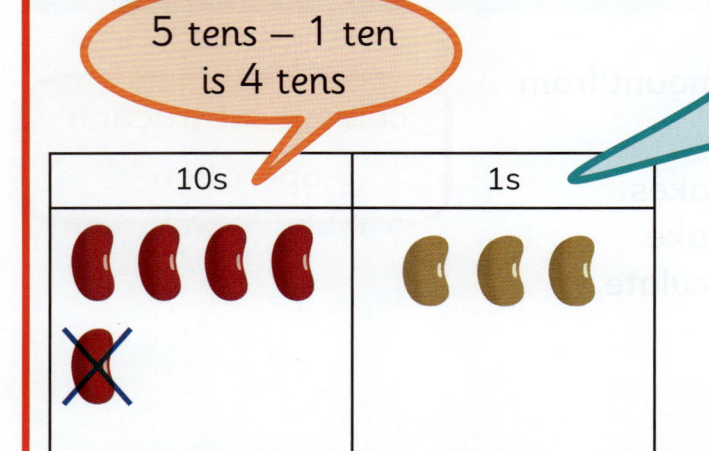

53 − 10 = ☐

5 tens − 1 ten is 4 tens

The ones have not changed. 53 − 10 = 43

| 10s | 1s |

Jump back 10 on the number line. 53 − 10 = 43

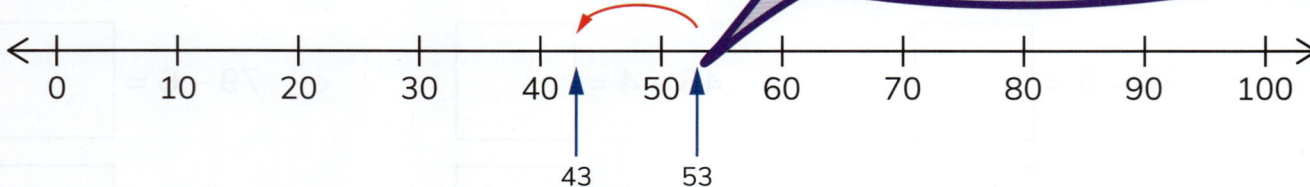

−10

0   10   20   30   40   50   60   70   80   90   100

43   53

Answer: 53 − 10 = 43

86

5.2 Subtraction

3 Find the missing numbers.

a 47 − 10 = ☐   b 85 − 10 = ☐   c 69 − 10 = ☐

d 36 − 20 = ☐   e 58 − 20 = ☐   f 64 − 30 = ☐

4 Find the missing numbers.

a   52   b   61   c   45
   − 10   − 20   − 30

Let's investigate

Choose a row from the bottom half of a 100 square. Subtract 20 from each of your numbers. What do you notice about your answers? Will the same thing happen, whichever row you choose?
Share your ideas with your partner.

5 Working with numbers to 100

5 Choose the correct operation (add or subtract) to solve each word problem. Write and solve your number sentence.

   a Dad bought a bag of 24 red apples and a bag of 10 green apples.

      How many apples did Dad buy? _____

   b There are 64 seats on the bus.

      30 people get on.

      How many empty seats are there? _____

   c There are 28 pages in Arun's book.

      He read 6 pages.

      How many pages does he have left to read? _____

   d A baker made 32 chocolate cookies and 20 raspberry cookies.

      How many cookies did he make altogether? _____

6 Tick the correct calculations. Correct any mistakes.

83 − 30	58 − 5	34 + 20	42 + 7
83	58	34	42
− 30	− 5	− 20	+ 7
53	8	14	49

Are some mistakes in question 6 easier to notice than others?

Why do you think that might be?

5.3 Multiplication

7   Draw a ring around the calculation that does not have the same answer as the others.

39 – 6   23 + 10   43 – 20   37 – 4

> **Look what I can do!**
>
> - I can subtract ones from a 2-digit number.
> - I can subtract tens from a 2-digit number.
> - I can choose when to add or subtract to solve a word problem.

> 5.3 Multiplication

> **We are going to …**
>
> - add equal groups
> - explore multiplication as equal addition and as an array
> - build the multiplication tables for 1, 2, 5 and 10.

When things come in equal groups, we can multiply to find out how many. Arrays help you to see equal groups, like on a muffin tray.

> array   equal groups
> multiply, times, multiplication
> repeated addition
> times table, multiplication table

89

Exercise 5.3

1 Write the repeated addition and multiplication number sentences.

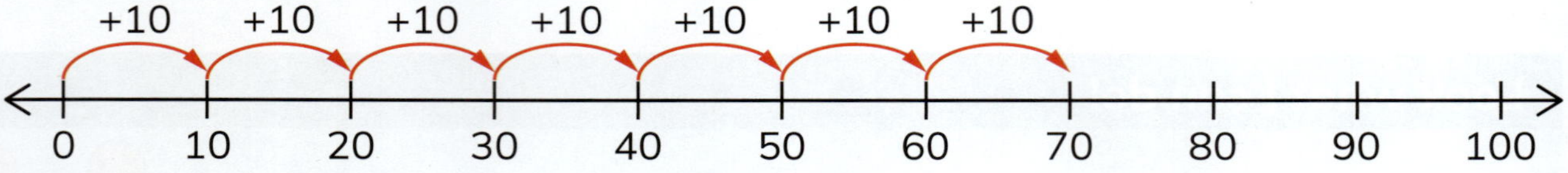

2 Show this repeated addition number sentence on the number line.

2 + 2 + 2 + 2 + 2 + 2 + 2 + 2 = 16

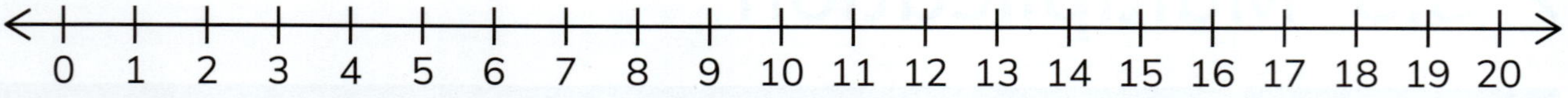

Write the multiplication number sentence.

3 Write the missing number sentences.

Repeated addition	Multiplication
5 + 5 + 5 + 5 + 5 = 25	
	2 × 4 = 8
10 + 10 + 10 + 10 + 10 = 50	
	5 × 3 = 15
2 + 2 + 2 + 2 + 2 = 10	
	10 × 2 = 20

4 Write a multiplication sentence for each array.

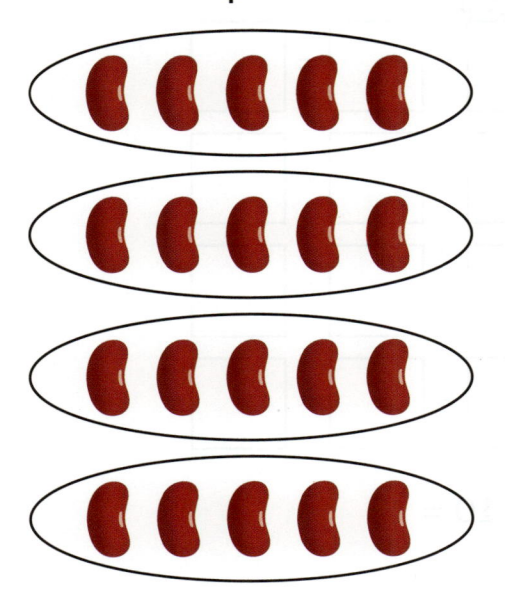

_____   _____

5 Draw an array to show that 2 × 8 = 16.

5 Working with numbers to 100

6   Write the multiplication table for 1, to 1 × 10 = 10.

1 × 1 = 1

☐ × ☐ = ☐

☐ × ☐ = ☐

☐ × ☐ = ☐

☐ × ☐ = ☐

☐ × ☐ = ☐

☐ × ☐ = ☐

☐ × ☐ = ☐

☐ × ☐ = ☐

1 × 10 = 10

> What helps you to remember a multiplication table?
> Are some multiplication tables easier to remember than others?
> Why is that? Discuss your ideas with your partner or in a small group.

Let's investigate

Write the multiplication table for 0.

How is this the same as any other multiplication table? How is it different? Discuss your ideas in a small group.

5.3 Multiplication

7 Write the missing double, addition and multiplication sentences.

Double	Addition	Multiplication
double 5 is 10		
	2 + 2 = 4	
		10 × 2 = 20

8 Use the counting stick to help you find the correct answers.

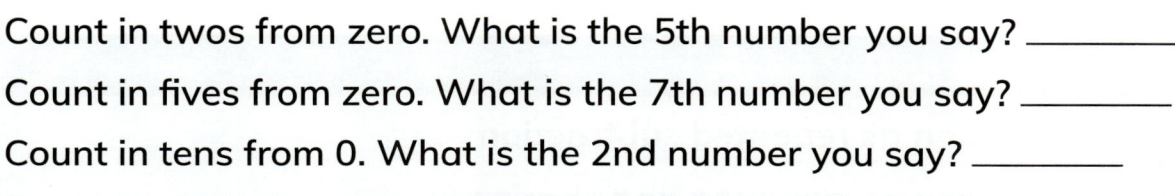

Count in twos from zero. What is the 5th number you say? _____

Count in fives from zero. What is the 7th number you say? _____

Count in tens from 0. What is the 2nd number you say? _____

Count in twos from 0. What is the 8th number you say? _____

9 Marcus likes to count in twos, fives and tens from zero. When he says '20', what could he be counting in?

Write some multiplication facts to explain your answer.

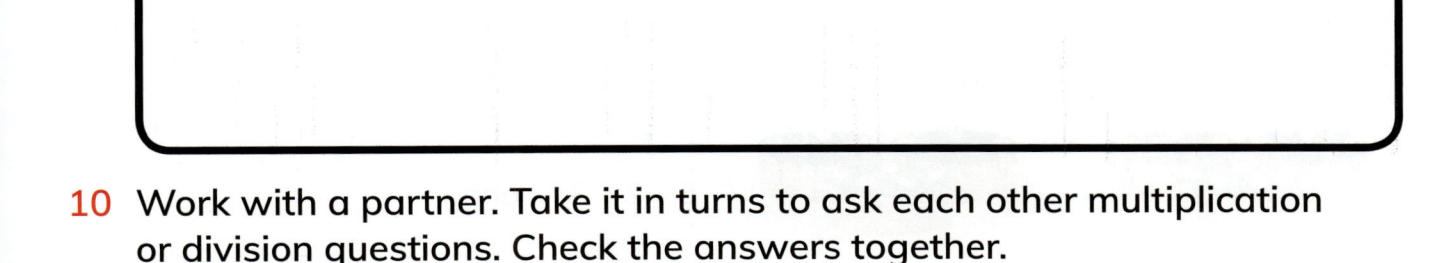

10 Work with a partner. Take it in turns to ask each other multiplication or division questions. Check the answers together.

5 Working with numbers to 100

Look what I can do!

- I can add equal groups.
- I can understand multiplication as repeated groups and as an array.
- I can record the multiplication tables for 1, 2, 5 and 10.

> 5.4 Division

We are going to ...

- explore division as repeated subtraction
- explore division as grouping and sharing
- decide whether to add or subtract to solve a word problem.

When we know the whole, we use division to find out how many equal groups we can make or how to share equally.

division, divide
division as grouping
division as sharing
repeated subtraction

Put 6 buns into groups of 2:

6 ÷ 2 = 3, grouping

Share 6 buns equally between 2 plates:

6 ÷ 2 = 3, sharing

5.4 Division

Exercise 5.4

1. Use repeated subtraction on the number line to help you solve each division.

   a   45 ÷ 5 = ☐

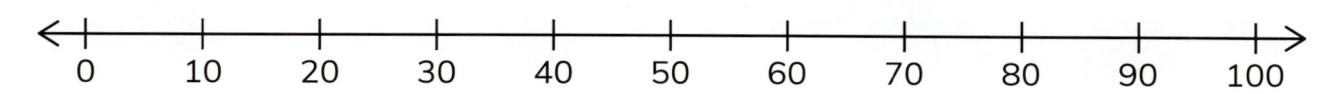

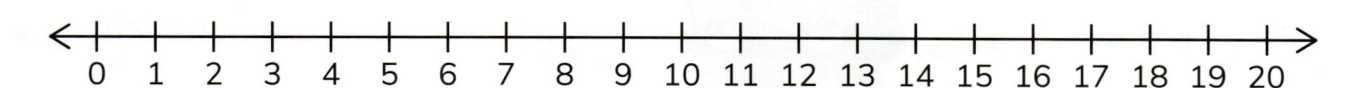

   0 10 20 30 40 50 60 70 80 90 100

   b   14 ÷ 2 = ☐

   0 1 2 3 4 5 6 7 8 9 10 11 12 13 14 15 16 17 18 19 20

2. Use the arrays to help you solve each division.

   Tip
   Use the groups of 5 and groups of 2 to help you.

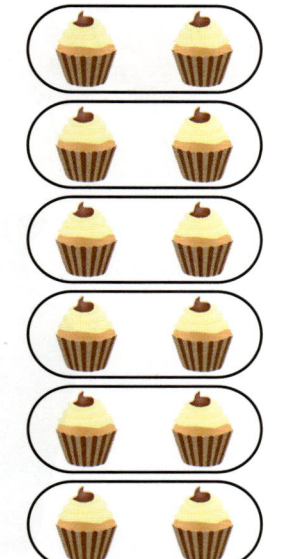

   a   35 ÷ 5 = ☐   b   12 ÷ 2 = ☐

5 Working with numbers to 100

Worked example 4

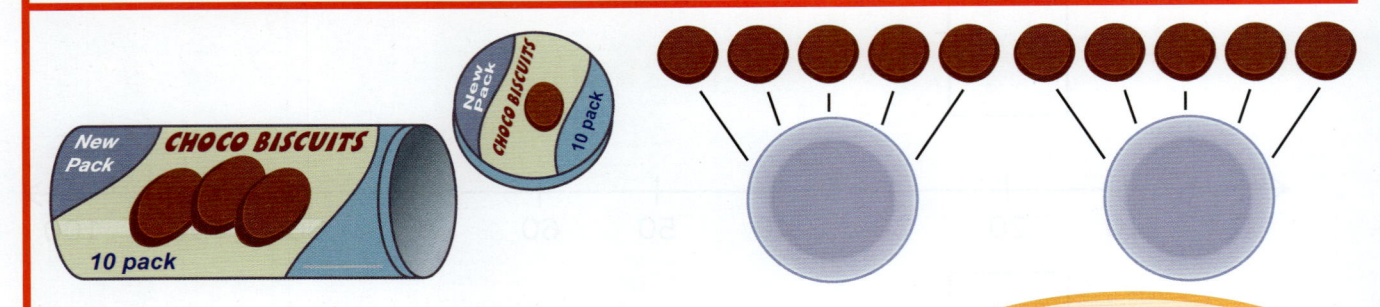

10 ÷ 2 = ☐

There are 2 plates.

Keep putting 1 on each plate until there are none left.

5 on each plate, 10 ÷ 2 = 5

Answer: 10 ÷ 2 = 5

3 Share the flowers between two vases.

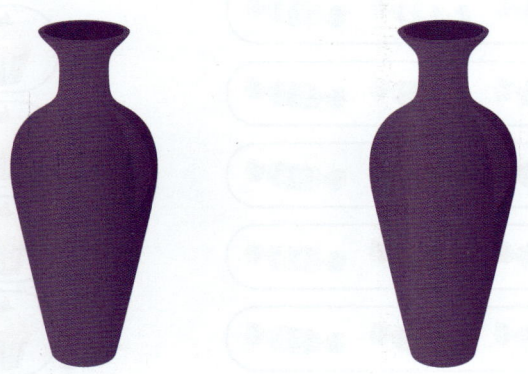

20 ÷ 2 = ☐

5.4 Division

4   Share the strawberries between 5 children.

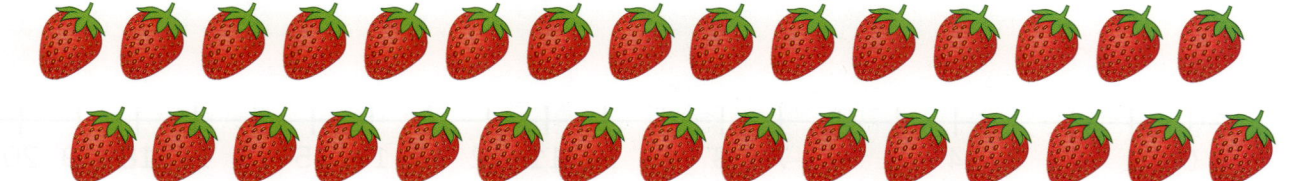

30 ÷ 5 = ☐

5   Write a division number sentence for each array.

Tip

Put the frogs and the wheels into groups to help you.

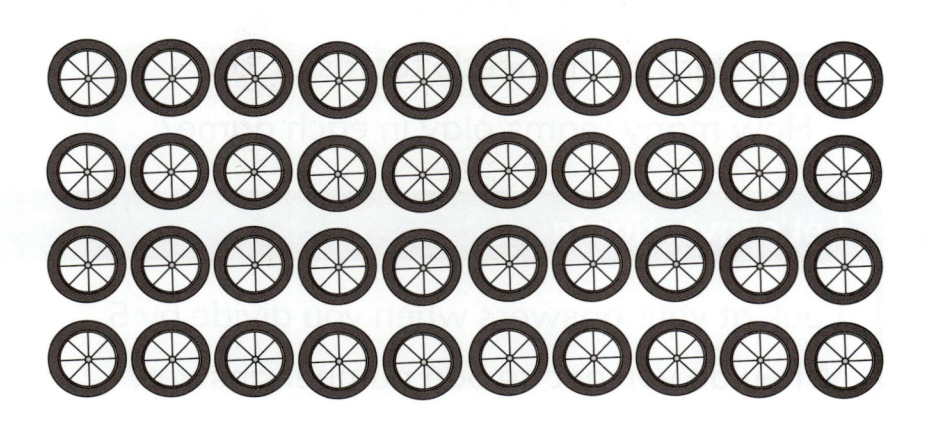

_____

_____

5 Working with numbers to 100

6 Choose a method to use and find the answers.

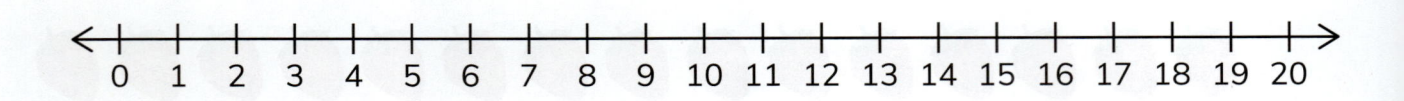

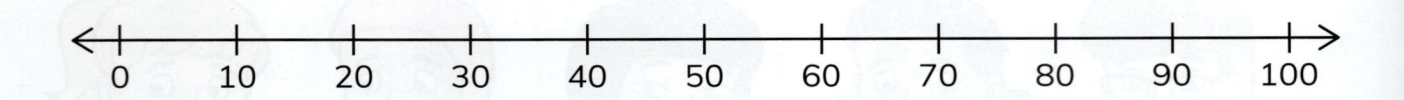

a 80 ÷ 10 = ☐   b 25 ÷ 5 = ☐   c 18 ÷ 2 = ☐

0 1 2 3 4 5 6 7 8 9 10 11 12 13 14 15 16 17 18 19 20

0 10 20 30 40 50 60 70 80 90 100

> Which method for division do you prefer (repeated subtraction, grouping or sharing)? Give at least 2 reasons for your answer.

7 30 children are playing some games.

The first game needs teams of 2.

The second game needs teams of 5.

The third game needs teams of 10.

How many teams play in each game?

Let's investigate

Look at your answers when you divide by 5.

When do you get an odd number answer?

When do you get an even number answer?

Explain why. Discuss your ideas with your partner.

5.4 Division

8   Write and solve the number sentences. Do you need to multiply or divide?

   a   5 children can sit on a bench. How many benches are needed for 30 children?

   b   10 children have 5 marbles each. How many marbles do they have altogether?

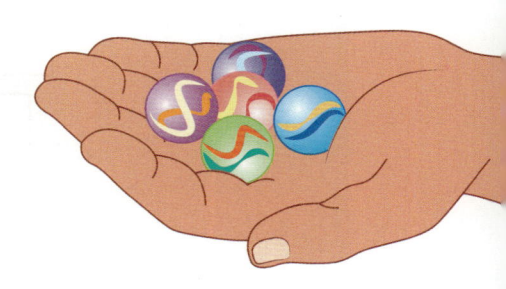

> Talk to a partner about how you decide whether to multiply or divide to solve a word problem.

Look what I can do!

- I can use repeated subtraction to solve a division number sentence.
- I can use grouping and sharing to solve a division number sentence.
- I can decide whether to multiply or divide to solve a word problem.

5 **Working with numbers to 100**

Check your progress

1 Find the missing totals.

   a   42
      + 5

   b   78
      + 10

   c   64
      + 30

   d   48
      − 20

   e   69
      − 10

   f   77
      − 6

2 Find the missing numbers. Use the number lines to help you.

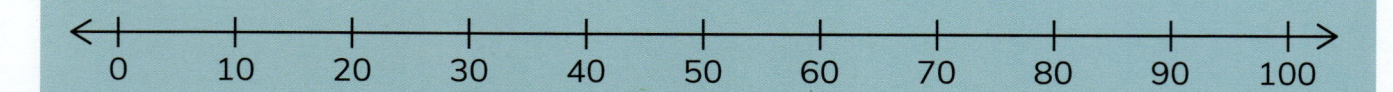

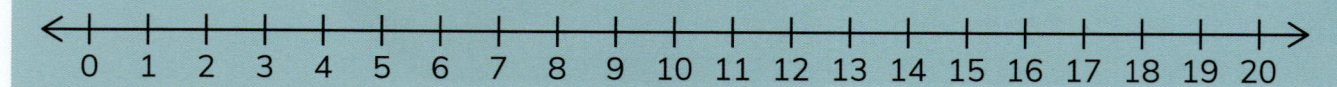

   a $3 \times 5 =$ ☐
   b $40 \div 10 =$ ☐
   c $9 \times 2 =$ ☐

   d $14 \div 2 =$ ☐
   e $1 \times 10 =$ ☐
   f $35 \div 5 =$ ☐

⟵—0—10—20—30—40—50—60—70—80—90—100⟶

⟵—0—1—2—3—4—5—6—7—8—9—10—11—12—13—14—15—16—17—18—19—20⟶

3 Write the number sentence you use to solve each problem.
   a There are 37 children in Class 2 when everyone is here, but 5 children are away. How many children in Class 2 today?

   b 5 horses share 20 carrots. How many carrots does each horse get?

Project 3: Borrowing pencils

> Project 3

Borrowing pencils

On Monday, a class of children are drawing some pictures. There is a tray of 68 colouring pencils at the front of the classroom. One child from each table goes up to the tray to borrow some pencils.

- Zara takes 10 pencils for her table.
- Arun takes 20 pencils for his table.
- Sofia takes 7 pencils for her table.
- Marcus takes 10 pencils for his table.

How many pencils are left in the tray?
How do you know?

At the end of the lesson, all of the children put back the pencils that they had borrowed. How many pencils are in the tray now?

On Tuesday, the class are making some posters. There is a pot of 39 marker pens at the front of the classroom. Zara, Arun, Sofia and Marcus all go up to the pot to borrow some pens. When they go back to their tables, there are 10 pens left in the pot.

How many pens could each person have taken? Is there more than one answer?

6 Money

Getting started

1. Sofia sorted some coins in two different ways.

   Label the coins in the circle.

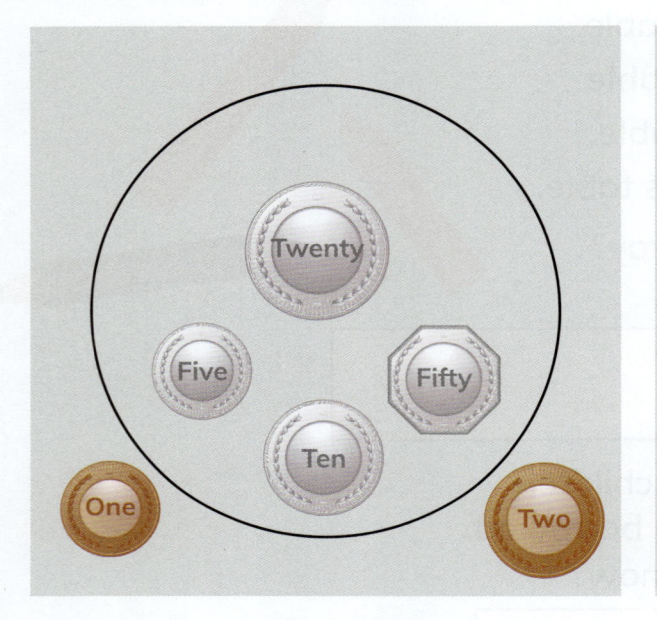

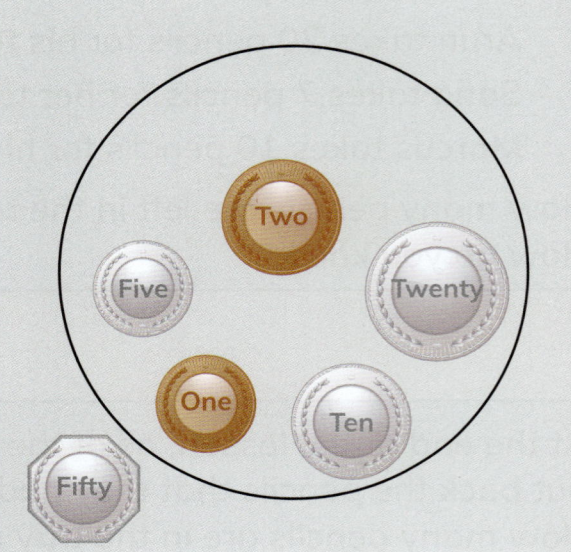

2. Here is the pattern Zara made with some coins.

   Five, Ten, Five, Ten, Five, Ten, Five, Ten

   Make a pattern with some coins. Use the circles to record your coin pattern.

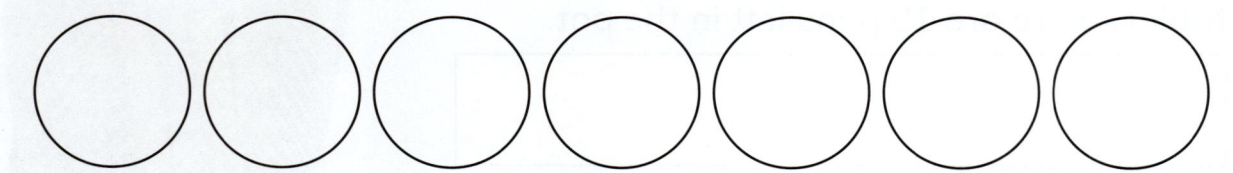

6 Money

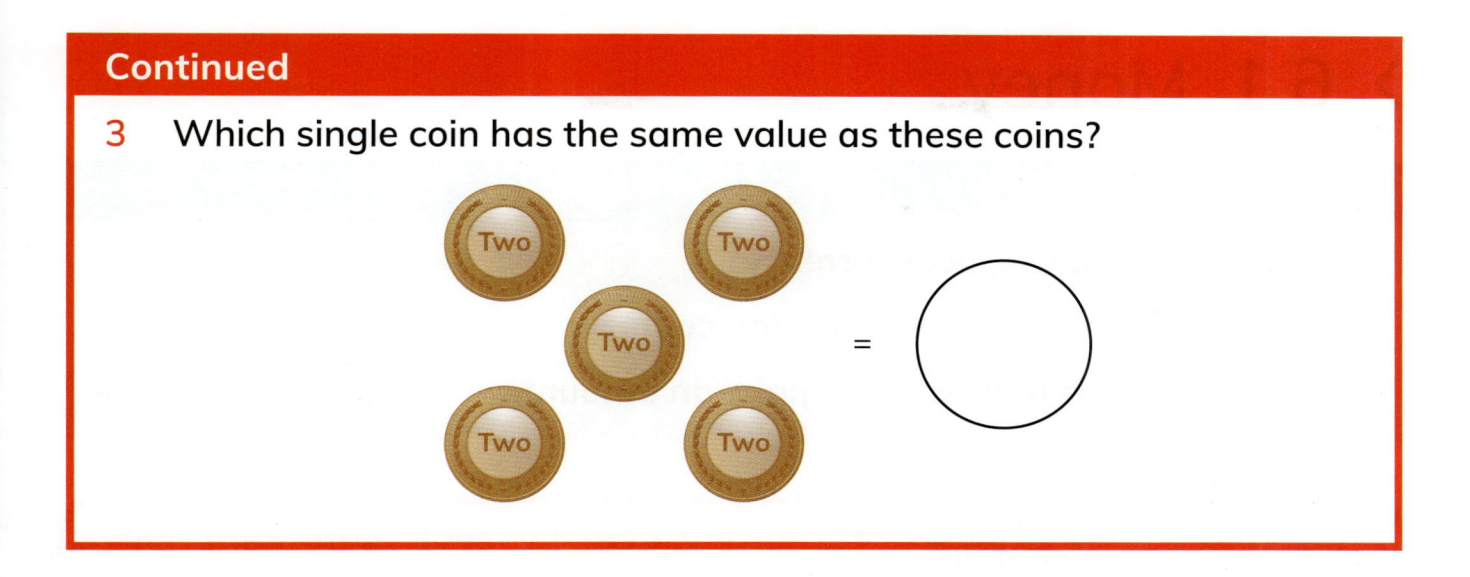

Continued

3   Which single coin has the same value as these coins?

Two   Two
   Two
Two   Two   =   ◯

We use money to buy the things we need or want.
Coins and banknotes have their value written on them.

Many countries have their own currency. In this unit, you will explore US currency. You will also explore your own currency, if it is different.

6 Money

> 6.1 Money

We are going to ...
- recognise and use local currency
- recognise and use US dollars and cents
- use banknotes and coins to make an amount.

Coins and banknotes have their value written on them. Different values can be used together to buy things.

currency   dollar, cent   euro, euro cent
pound, pence   price
unit of money   value   worth   yen

Exercise 6.1

Tip
A dollar is worth 100 cents.

1 How many cents is each of these coins worth?

Coin		Value in cents
Penny		1
Nickel		
Dime		
Quarter dollar		
Half dollar		

6.1 Money

2. Which single coin is worth the same as each row of coins?
Draw or write your answer.

2 nickels	
2 quarters	
5 nickels	
5 dimes	
5 pennies	
11 nickels	

Work with your partner to write and answer a question like this one about your own currency.

_____

_____

3. Marcus spent 50c on some candy.

He did not have a half dollar coin.

Which other coins could he pay with?

105

6 Money

> **Let's investigate**
>
> Zara says there must be at least 10 different ways to make 20c.
> Do you agree? How many different ways can you find?
> Check your ways to make 20c with your partner.

4 Zara spent US$25 on a T-shirt.
   Which banknotes could she pay with?

> **Tip**
>
> There are US banknotes for $1, $2, $5, $10, $20, $50 and $100.

> **Let's investigate**
>
> You have 2 different banknotes.
> Each banknote is less than US$100. How much could you have?
> Have you found all the possible answers?
> Share your ways to make US$100 with your partner.

5 Arun spent US$8 and 60c in the supermarket.
   Which banknotes and coins could he pay with?

6.1 Money

6 Find the total amount of money in each row and each column.
Two answers have been completed for you.

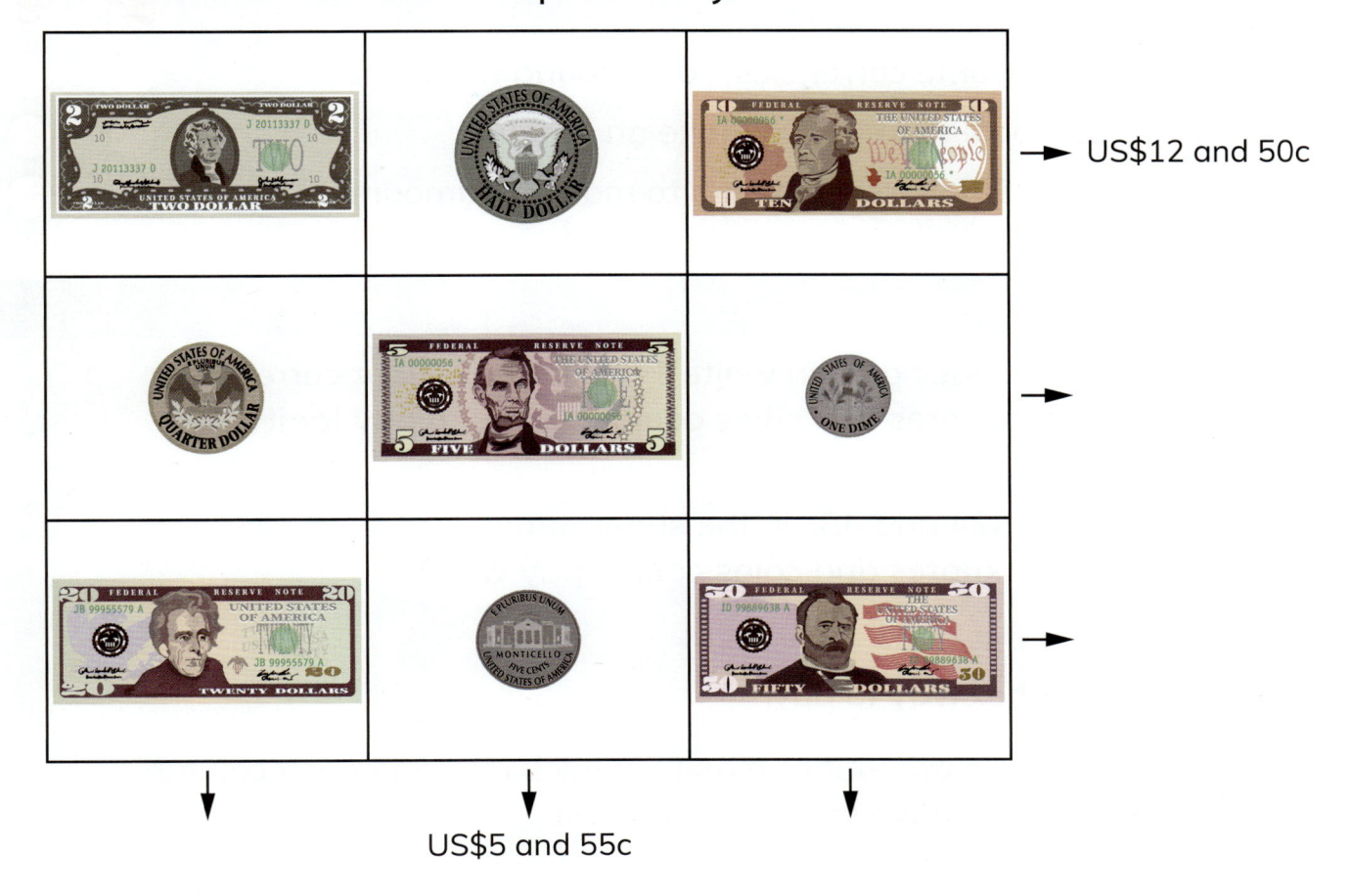

→ US$12 and 50c

↓ US$5 and 55c

> How is adding coins and banknotes together the same as adding numbers together? How is it different?

Let's investigate

Work with a partner.

Take it in turns to think of a US coin or banknote. Ask your partner questions, for example, 'Is it a coin?' 'Is it worth more than a dime?' Your partner can only answer yes or no.

Can you identify the coin or banknote after 3 questions?

6 Money

Look what I can do!

- I recognise some currencies from around the world.
- I can use local currency to make an amount.
- I can use US dollars and cents to make an amount.

Check your progress

1. How much does a plain white T-shirt cost in your currency?
   Which banknotes and coins could you use to pay for it?

2. I spent US$24 and 45c in the supermarket.
   Which banknotes and coins could I pay with?

   Find another way to pay.

3. Find the total amount of money in each row and each column.
   Two answers have been done for you.

$20 note	1c coin	$1 note	→ US$21 and 1c
5c coin	$50 note	half dollar coin	→
half dollar coin	$5 note	1 dime coin	→

↓ US$55 and 1c ↓ ↓

108

7 Time

Getting started

1. The days of the week and months of the year are mixed up together.

   On a separate piece of paper, try to write them in the correct order.

   Wednesday   Sunday   December
   May   October   June
   January   February   Tuesday
   Thursday   Saturday
   April   September
   August   Monday   Friday
   March
   July   November

2. What day is today? _____

   What day is tomorrow? _____

   What day was yesterday? _____

3. Write the correct month in each box.

Last month	This month	Next month

7 Time

We use different units to measure time. In everyday life, a second is the shortest unit of time and a year is the longest.

A calendar shows us an arrangement of days and months usually for 1 year.

> 7.1 Units of time and the calendar

> **We are going to ...**
> - order and compare units of time
> - record dates in numbers and words
> - read the date from a calendar.

Time is constantly passing. We need to have an idea of how long things take to plan what we do. We also need to know how to read and write dates so that we can be where we need to be on any day.

> calendar   date   second   units of time   weekend   year

Exercise 7.1

1 Name 3 things that take about a second.

2 Name 3 things that take about a minute or just a few minutes.

3 Put these units of time in order from the shortest to the longest.

   | month | minute | day | hour | week |

7 Time

4 Draw a line to match the units of time that are the same.

Tip
Use a calendar to help you.

| 1 year | 1 month | 1 week | 1 hour |

| 60 minutes | 7 days | 12 months | about 4 weeks |

5 Write these dates in numbers only.

The day after Tuesday 4th January 2022

The day before Saturday 2nd February 2019

6 Write the circled dates in words.

FEBRUARY 2021

M	T	W	T	F	S	S
1	2	3	4	5	6	7
8	9	10	11	12	13	14
15	16	17	18	19	20	21
22	23	24	(25)	26	27	28

MARCH 2021

M	T	W	T	F	S	S
1	2	3	4	5	6	7
8	9	10	11	12	13	14
15	(16)	17	18	19	20	21
22	23	24	25	26	27	28
29	30	31				

_____

_____

_____

Tip
Remember to write the day when you write the date in words.

112

7.1 Units of time and the calendar

> **Let's investigate**
>
> February is the only month with 28 days, 29 in a leap year.
>
> All the other months have 30 or 31 days.
>
> Is there a pattern to how many days there are in each month?
>
> Discuss with your partner.

7 Look at this year's calendar.

In which months will you find these dates?

Monday 4th

Wednesday 18th

Saturday 23rd

> Talk to your partner about how you found your answers to question 7. Did you work in the same way or a different way to your partner? Would you try a different way of working if you did the same activity again?

Look what I can do!

- I can order and compare units of time.
- I can read and interpret the information in a calendar.
- I can record dates in numbers and words.

7 Time

Check your progress

1. Here are some units of time.

   | day | week | hour | month |

   The shortest unit is _____

   The longest unit is _____

2. Here is the calendar for October 2022.

   OCTOBER

M	T	W	T	F	S	S
					1	2
③	4	5	6	7	8	9
10	11	12	13	14	15	16
17	18	19	20	㉑	22	23
24	25	㉖	27	28	29	30
31						

   Write the ringed dates in words and numbers.

   _____

   _____

   _____

3. What day of the week is 01/11/22?

   _____

   What day of the week is 30/09/22?

   _____

   Tip
   Use the calendar in question 2 to help you.

Project 4

Time a task

For this activity you will need to work in pairs.

One of you will use a timer that shows seconds, and the other will choose one of the following tasks:

a   Counting to 20
b   Drawing a simple stick man
c   Standing on one foot for as long as possible
d   Saying a nursery rhyme
e   Walking slowly round the room

The person who has the timer will set the stopwatch to zero and then time how long it takes for the other to do the chosen task. Remember to say 'GO!' as you start the timer and to stop it as soon as your partner finishes the task.

Make a note of how long that task took, then swap over and repeat the same task.

You could then each try another task and write down the times taken.

Now you're going to estimate how long you think the following tasks will take before you time yourselves:

a   Saying the alphabet
b   Counting to 100
c   Writing the numbers 1 to 10 clearly

Write down the estimate and then see how close you are when you are timed.

How are you making your estimates each time?

8 Numbers to 100 (2)

Getting started

1. Split each number into tens and ones.

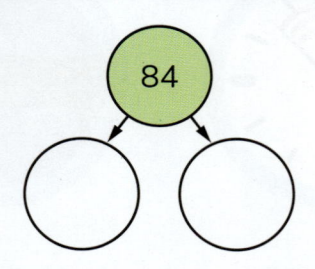

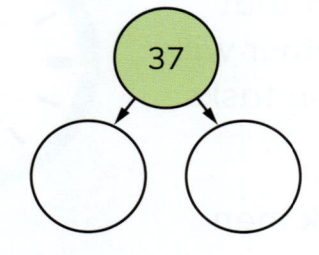

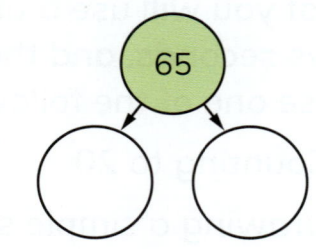

   84   37   65

2. Share 20 strawberries between 5 bowls.

   Complete the division number sentence.

   20 ÷ 5 = ☐

3. Tick the shapes that show quarters.

   A 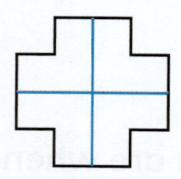   B 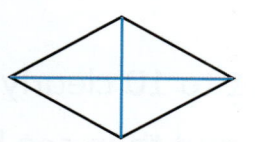   C

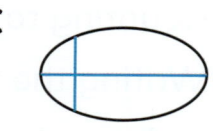

   D 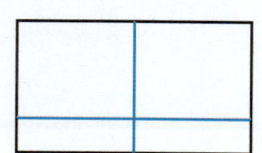   E 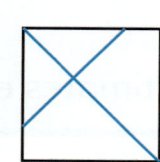   F

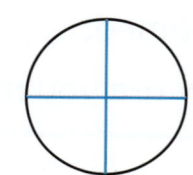

8 Numbers to 100 (2)

In this unit you will use place value in new ways.

You will split numbers in different ways. You will also use what you know about fractions of shapes to find fractions of numbers.

Sharing things fairly, using fractions or division, is something you will need to do often.

24 hats

We need 24 party hats. That's 20 and 4.

Or 10, 10 and 4.

117

8 Numbers to 100 (2)

> 8.1 Numbers in words, rounding and regrouping

We are going to …
- write 2-digit numbers in words
- round 2-digit numbers to the nearest 10
- regroup 2-digit numbers in different ways.

Sometimes numbers are written in words. You need to read and understand numbers and number words.

> closest 10
> hyphen
> nearest 10
> regroup
> round, rounding

Exercise 8.1

1   Write in words each of the numbers represented.

   a

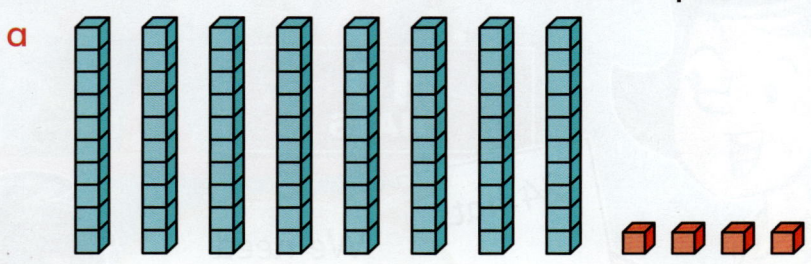

   _____

   b

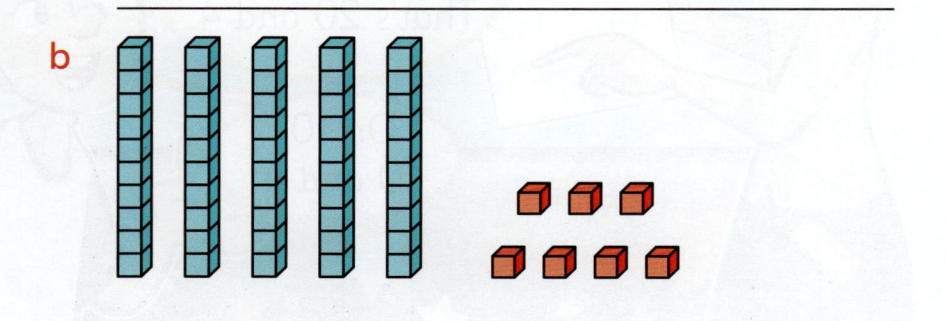

   _____

   c   93 _____

   d   31 _____

118

8.1 Numbers in words, rounding and regrouping

2   Read the number words and write the number.

   a   forty-two   _____

   b   seventy-six   _____

   c   twenty-five   _____

   d   sixty-eight   _____

3   Use these number words to write some 2-digit numbers in words. How many different numbers can you write?

   twenty   seventy   forty   eight   nine

   _____

   _____

   _____

   _____

> How does understanding place value help you to write a number in words? Discuss with your partner or in a small group.

Let's investigate

Marcus says there is only one 2-digit number word with 12 letters, seventy-seven. Is Marcus correct?

8 Numbers to 100 (2)

> **Worked example 1**
>
> Round 74 to the nearest 10. 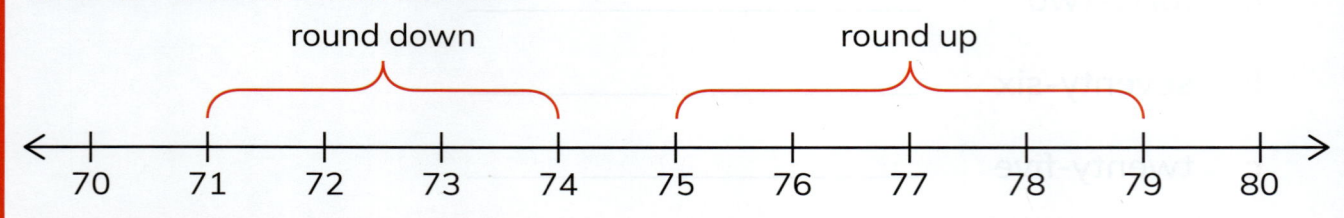
>
> round down — 71 72 73 74
> round up — 75 76 77 78 79
>
> 70 71 72 73 74 75 76 77 78 79 80
>
> 74 is closer to 70 than 80.
>
> 70 is the nearest 10, so 74 rounds to 70.
>
> **Answer:** 74 rounds to 70 when rounding to the nearest 10.

4 Round each number to the nearest 10.
Use the number line to help you.

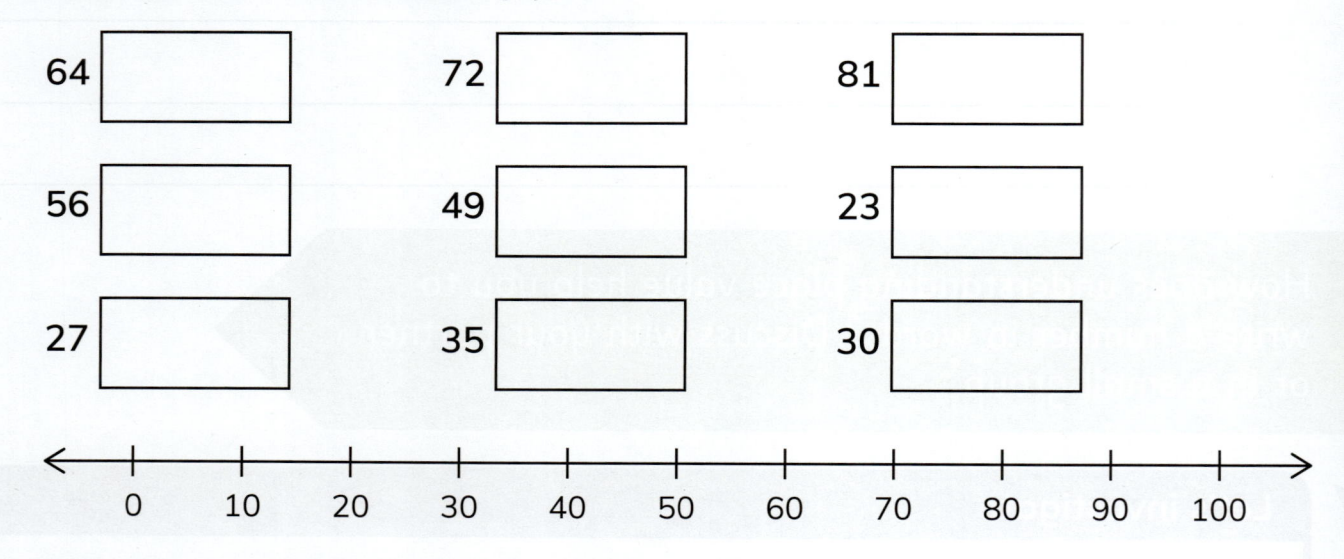

64 ☐   72 ☐   81 ☐

56 ☐   49 ☐   23 ☐

27 ☐   35 ☐   30 ☐

0 10 20 30 40 50 60 70 80 90 100

5 A number rounded to the nearest 10 is 60.
What could the number be?

120

8.1 Numbers in words, rounding and regrouping

6   Find 4 different ways to regroup 31. Draw or write your answers.

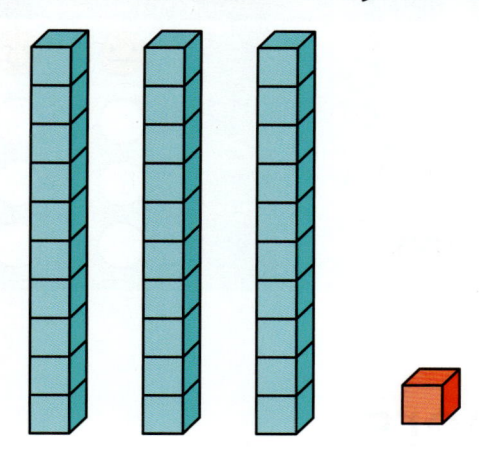

Compare the ways you regrouped 31 with a partner.
What did you do the same? What did you do differently?

How does understanding place value help you to regroup 2-digit numbers?

Let's investigate

Is Arun correct? If he is correct, will Arun's method always tell you how many different ways there are to regroup a number?

Discuss with a partner.

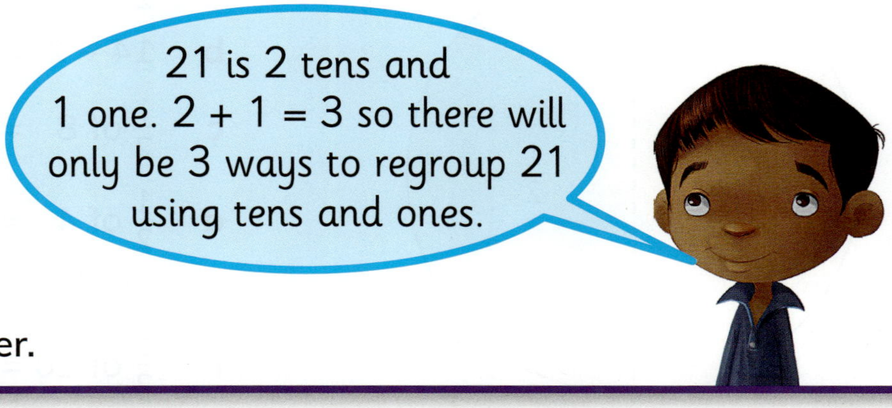

> 21 is 2 tens and 1 one. 2 + 1 = 3 so there will only be 3 ways to regroup 21 using tens and ones.

8 Numbers to 100 (2)

> **Look what I can do!**
>
> - I can write 2-digit numbers in words.
> - I can round 2-digit numbers to the nearest 10.
> - I can regroup 2-digit numbers in different ways.

> 8.2 Fractions of numbers

> **We are going to ...**
>
> - find half of an even number to 20
> - find a quarter of 4, 8, 12, 16 and 20
> - explore adding fractions.

Finding a fraction of a number is the same as dividing the whole by the denominator.

denominator
numerator
visualise

Exercise 8.2

1. Find the missing numbers.

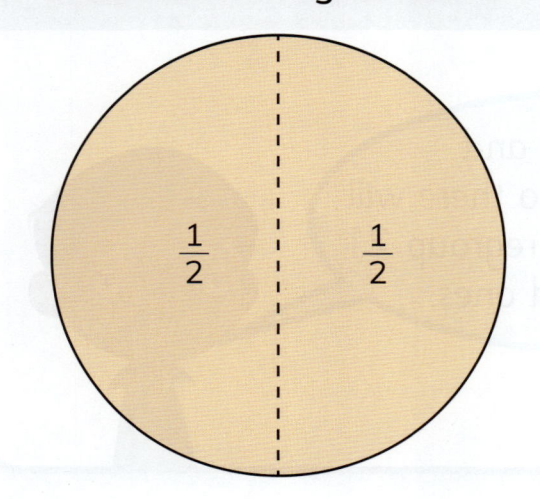

a $\frac{1}{2}$ of 10 = _____

b 14 ÷ 2 = _____

c $\frac{1}{2}$ of 8 = _____

d $\frac{1}{2}$ of 4 = _____

e 20 ÷ 2 = _____

f $\frac{1}{2}$ of 20 = _____

122

8.2 Fractions of numbers

What do you notice about finding a half and dividing by 2? Discuss with a partner or in a small group.

2   Complete the halves table.

Number	2	4	6	8	10	12	14	16	18	20
Half										

3   12 children made two equal teams.
    How many children are in each team?

Worked example 2

Half of a number is 4. What is the number?

Fold a square in half.
Open it up and put 4 counters on one half.

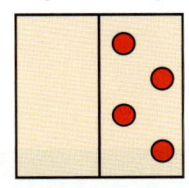

Visualise 4 counters on the other half
to make the whole. 8 counters altogether.

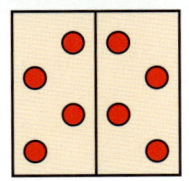

Answer: The number is 8.

4   Half of a number is 7. What is the number?

8 Numbers to 100 (2)

5   Find the missing numbers.

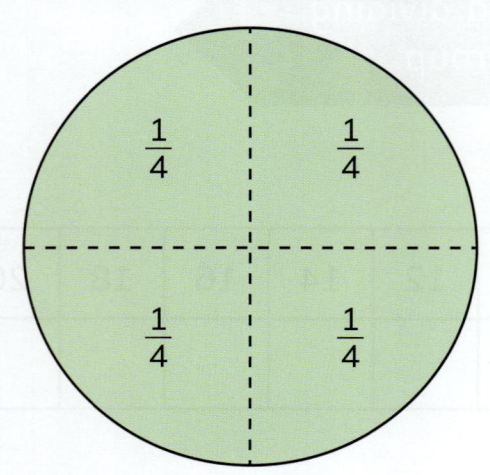

a $\frac{1}{4}$ of 12 = ☐

b   4 ÷ 4 = ☐

c $\frac{1}{4}$ of 8 = ☐

d   8 ÷ 4 = ☐

What does the 1 represent in $\frac{1}{2}$ and $\frac{1}{4}$? What is it called?

6   Marcus and his 3 brothers shared a bag of 8 apples equally.

a   How many apples did they each get?

b   What fraction of the whole did they each get?

How did you find the answers to question 6? Did you find a quarter or divide by 4? Discuss with a partner or in a small group.

7   A quarter of a number is 3. What is the number?

8   Complete the quarters table.

Number	4	8	12	16	20
Quarter					

8.2 Fractions of numbers

9 Tick the correct sentences.

$\frac{1}{2}$ of the children have long hair.

$\frac{1}{4}$ of the children have short hair.

Three-quarters of the children have long hair.

10 Find the missing fractions. Use the fractions of the square pictures to help you.

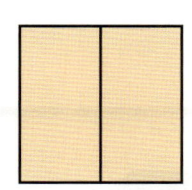

$\frac{1}{4} + \frac{1}{4} = \boxed{}$

$\frac{1}{2} + \frac{1}{4} + \boxed{} = 1$

$\frac{1}{4} + \frac{1}{4} + \frac{1}{4} + \boxed{} = 1$

$\frac{2}{2} = \frac{1}{2} + \boxed{}$

$\frac{4}{4} = \frac{1}{4} + \boxed{} + \boxed{} + \boxed{}$

8 Numbers to 100 (2)

Let's investigate

What do you think?

- A quarter of the Colombia flag is red.
- I can visualise the 4 quarters.
- No it isn't. The red is not one of four equal pieces.

Compare your investigation with a friend's. If you were going to do the investigation again, would you do anything different?

11 Choose a number. Find $\frac{1}{2}$ of your number. Then find $\frac{2}{4}$ of your number. Show that $\frac{1}{2}$ and $\frac{2}{4}$ are equivalent.

12 Label each of the marks on the number line. You could give more than one label to some marks.

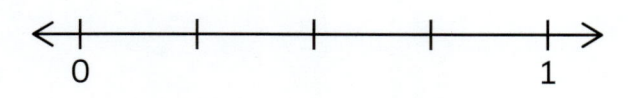

8.2 Fractions of numbers

Look what I can do!

- I can find half of an even number to 20.
- I can find a quarter of 4, 8, 12, 16 and 20.
- I can add fractions and recognise when fractions are equivalent.

Check your progress

1. Round each number to the nearest 10. Write your answer in words.

   a sixty-one: _____

   b forty-eight: _____

   c seventy-nine: _____

   d twenty-two: _____

   e forty-five: _____

   f seventy: _____

2. Sofia regrouped 58 in different ways. Continue her pattern of regrouping.

   50 + 8, 40 + 18,

3. Match each calculation to the correct value.

   $\frac{1}{2}$ of 8   2 $\frac{1}{4}$ of 16

   $\frac{4}{4}$ of 6   4 $\frac{2}{2}$ of 8

   $\frac{1}{2}$ of 4   6 $\frac{2}{4}$ of 12

   $\frac{2}{4}$ of 16   8 $\frac{1}{4}$ of 8

9 Statistics (2)

Getting started

1. You have 4 squares and 6 circles.
   Sort and sketch the shapes into the correct circles.

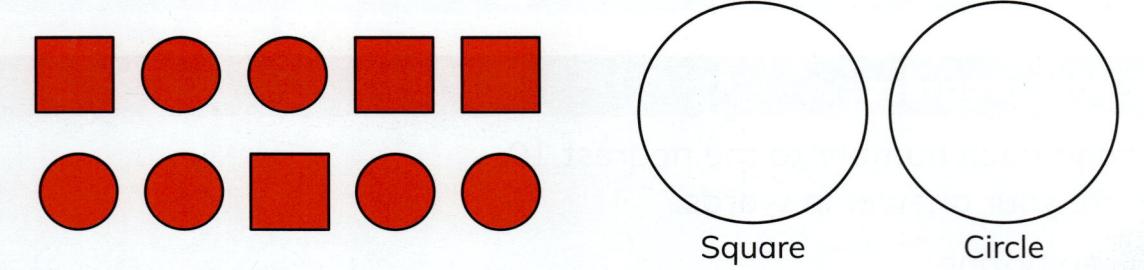

   Square   Circle

2. You have 5 squares and 7 triangles.
   Sort and sketch them into the correct circles.

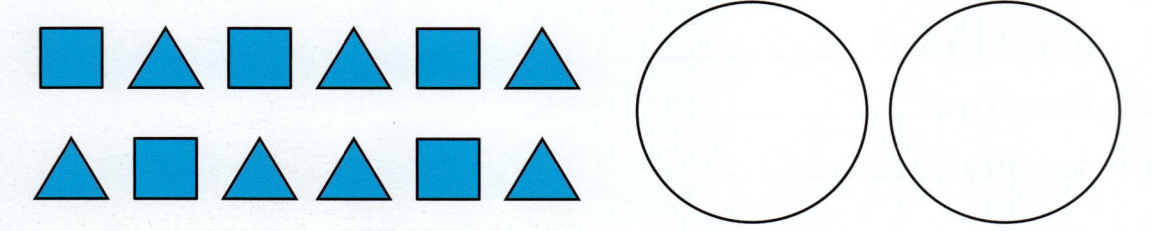

   Label your circles.

3. How many shapes are there altogether in questions 1 and 2?

   Which shapes are there more of?

   _____

   Which shapes are there fewer of?

   _____

   What is the difference between the number of most shapes and the number of fewest shapes?

   _____

   > **Tip**
   > Count the shapes in all 4 circles.

9 Statistics (2)

This unit will show you different ways to sort and show data so that you can choose the best way when you have collected information.

You will look again at Venn diagrams, lists and tables, pictograms and block graphs.

9 Statistics (2)

> 9.1 Venn diagrams, lists and tables

We are going to …
- collect data and record it using Venn diagrams, lists and tables
- describe the data and discuss results.

Lists and tables let you read or count data easily.
A Venn diagram uses rules to sort data into groups.

> Venn diagram

Worked example 1

Sort these shapes into the 2 circles.

Use the rule on the label. Use the letters next to each shape.

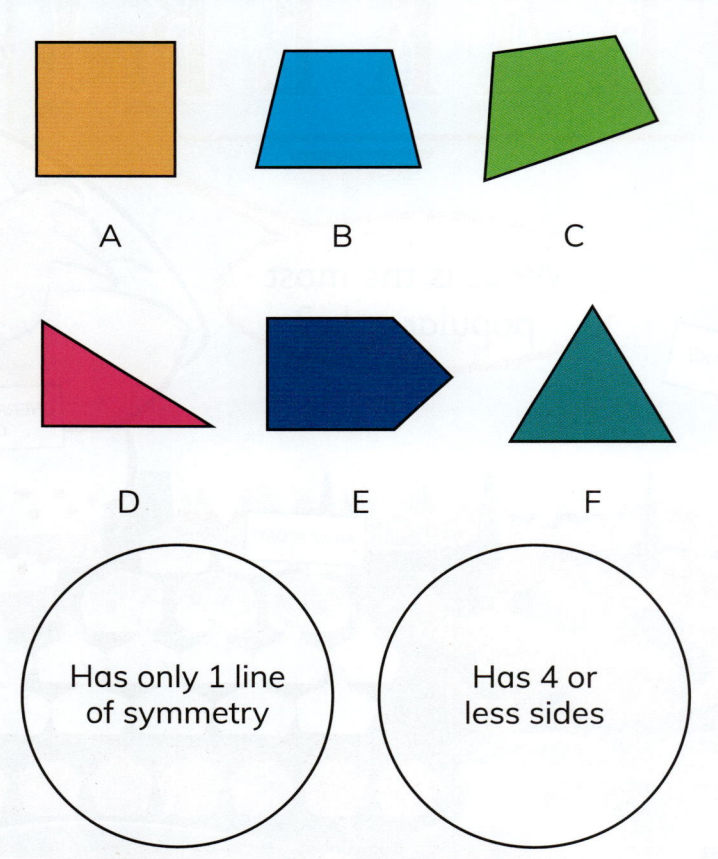

A B C

D E F

(Has only 1 line of symmetry)   (Has 4 or less sides)

9.1 Venn diagrams, lists and tables

Continued

I can see a shape that fits into both circles.

Which circle shall we put it in?

We can put part of one circle over the other and put the shape in the middle.

Answer:

Has only 1 line of symmetry
E

B

Has 4 or less sides
A C D F

131

Exercise 9.1

1 Look at this Venn diagram.

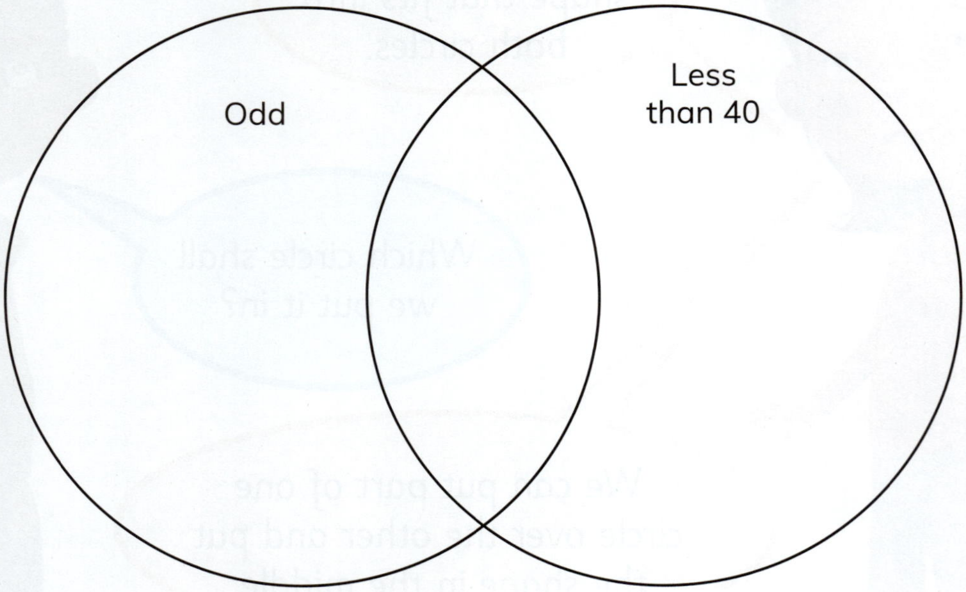

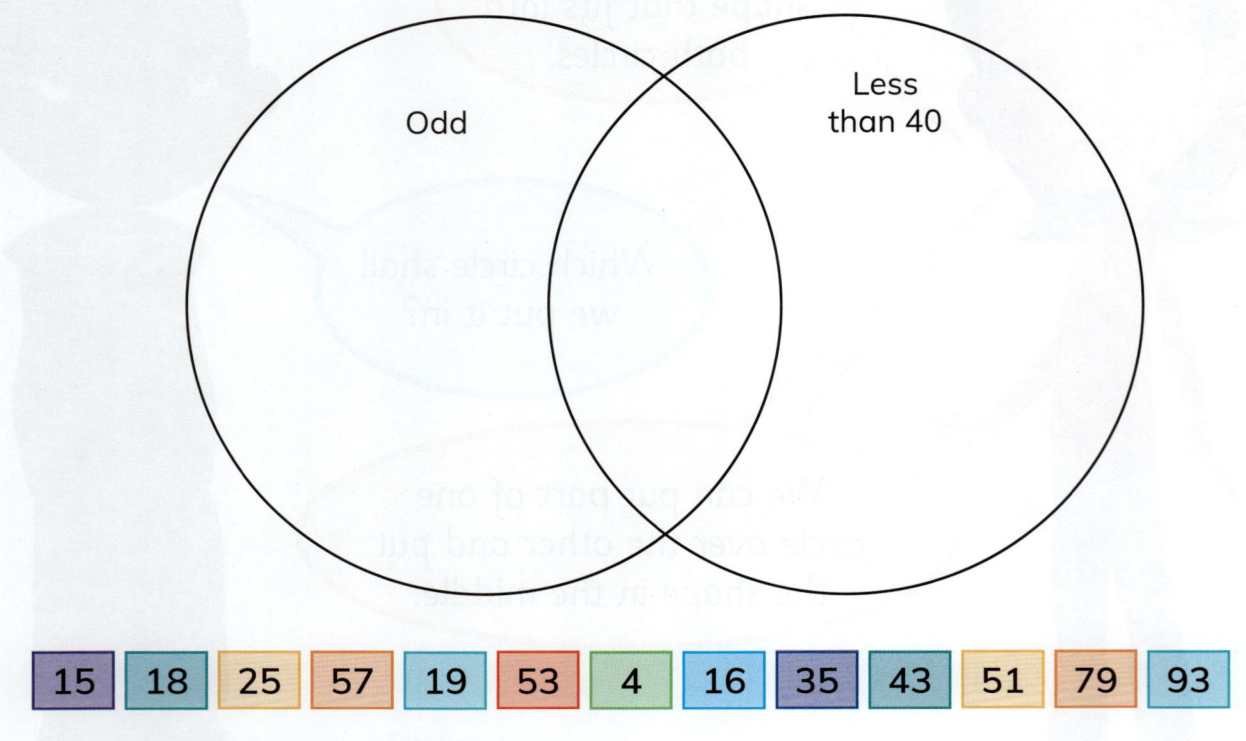

15 | 18 | 25 | 57 | 19 | 53 | 4 | 16 | 35 | 43 | 51 | 79 | 93

Write a list of the odd numbers.

___

Write a list of the numbers that are less than 40.

___

Write a list of the numbers that would go in the middle of the Venn diagram.

___

Now write your numbers in the Venn diagram above.

9.1 Venn diagrams, lists and tables

2   These children are playing a game.

Ana   Ben   Cyrus   Dina   Ed   Fiona

They are using large circles on the floor to put themselves into as many different groups as they can.

Find 3 different ways of sorting them.
Write the names into the Venn diagrams.

Don't forget to write the labels.

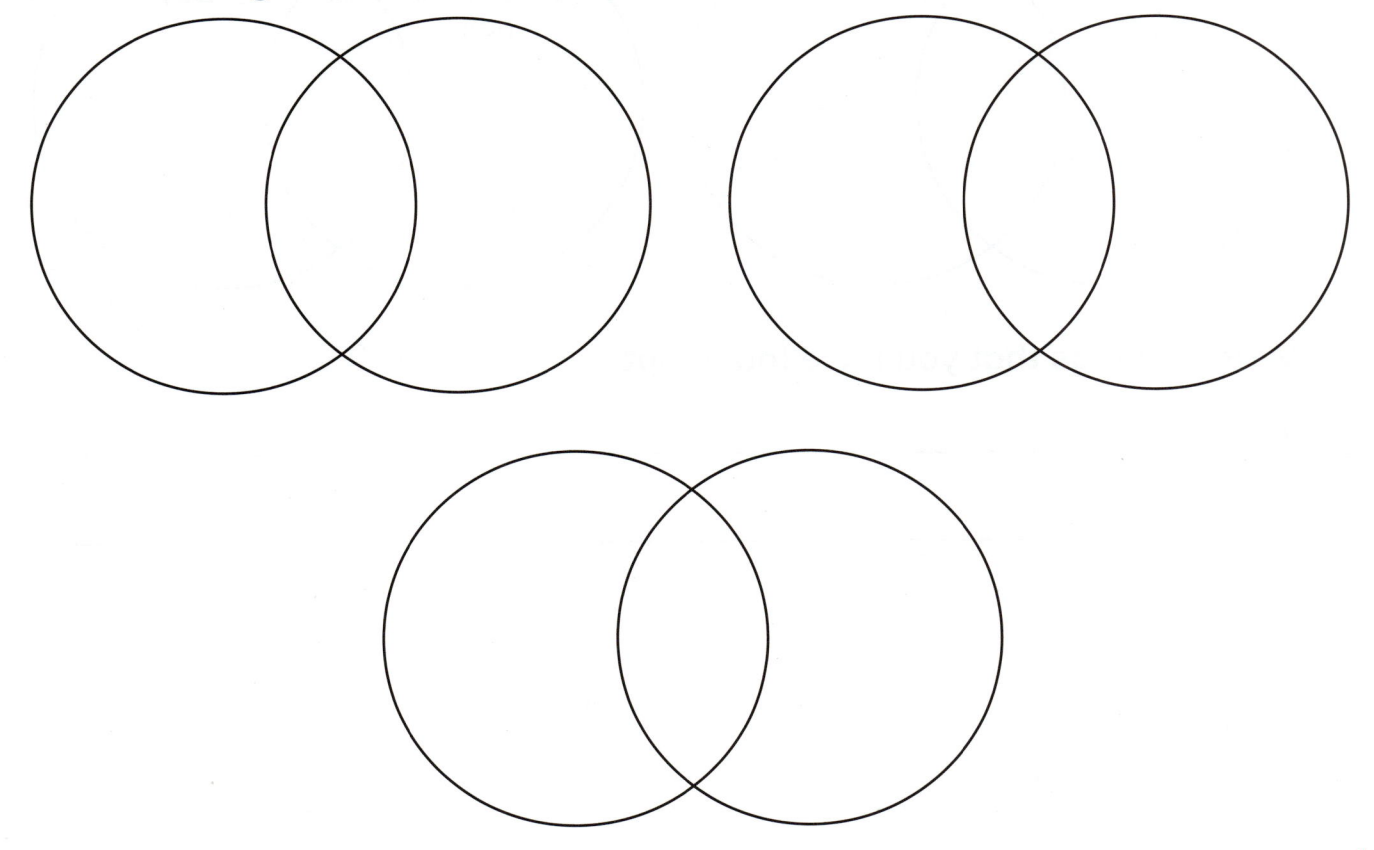

9 Statistics (2)

Describe what you did. Write 3 things the data tells you.

1 _____

2 _____

3 _____

3 Work with a partner.

Write the names of these children in the correct places in the Venn diagrams.

| Anika | Bakari | Jayleen | Tyler | Chyna | Anan | Joshua |

Wears glasses — Girl

Has blond hair — Boy

Write 2 things that you have found out.

1 _____

2 _____

9.1 Venn diagrams, lists and tables

4   Shapes are sorted into 2 sets.

How many shapes are red? ☐

How many shapes have 4 or fewer sides? ☐

How many shapes are there altogether? ☐

Venn diagram: Red (23), overlap (52), More than 4 sides (14)

Write another question about the data in the Venn diagram.
Give it to your partner to answer.

_____

5   Work as a group of 6 and choose one subject each from the list below.

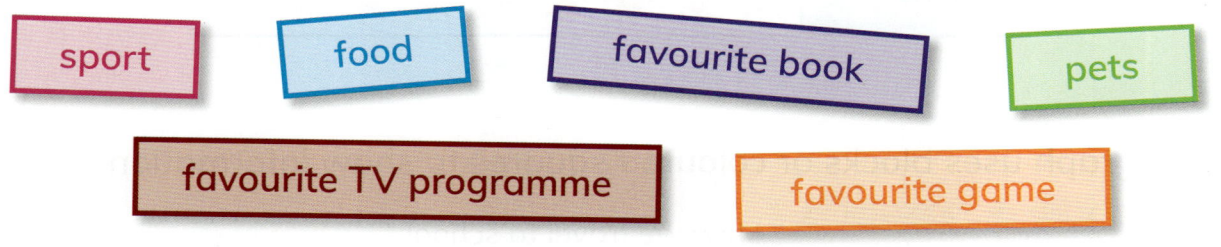

- sport
- food
- favourite book
- pets
- favourite TV programme
- favourite game

You will need some paper to write on.

Decide on a question to ask the others in your group.

Record the answers.

How will you show the data you have got? Explain your choice.

_____

Look what I can do!

- I can collect data and record it using Venn diagrams, lists and tables.
- I can describe the data and discuss results.

9 Statistics (2)

9.2 Pictograms and block graphs

We are going to ...
- collect data and record it using pictograms and block graphs
- describe the data and discuss results.

A pictogram uses simple drawings to represent data.

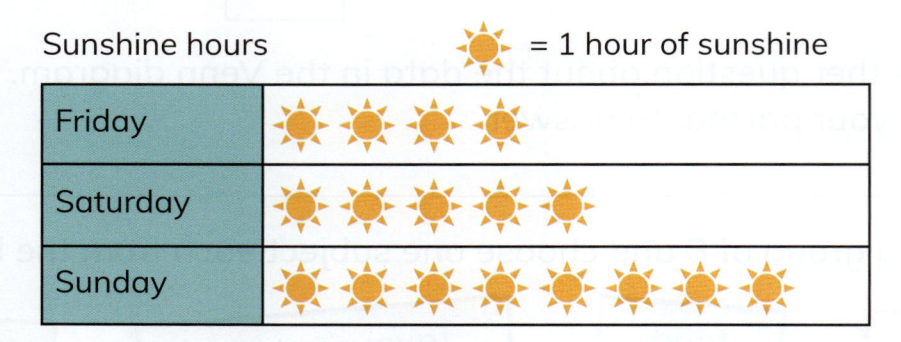

Sunshine hours ☀ = 1 hour of sunshine

Friday	☀ ☀ ☀ ☀
Saturday	☀ ☀ ☀ ☀ ☀
Sunday	☀ ☀ ☀ ☀ ☀ ☀ ☀ ☀

A block graph uses blocks or coloured squares to show information.

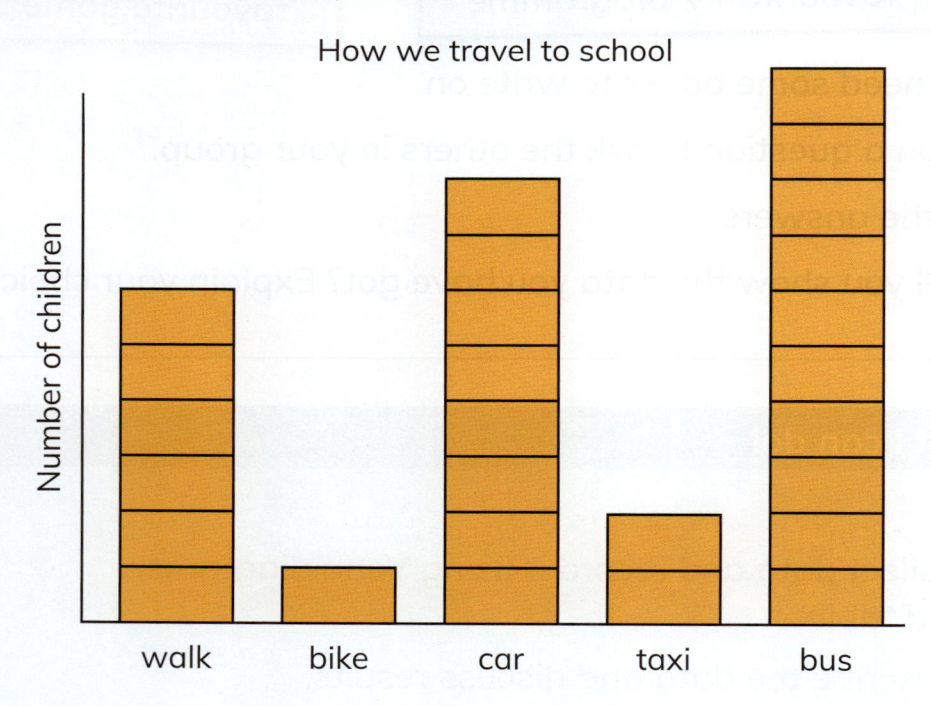

How we travel to school

(Block graph showing Number of children: walk, bike, car, taxi, bus)

9.2 Pictograms and block graphs

Exercise 9.2

1 This pictogram shows the cars parked in the car park.

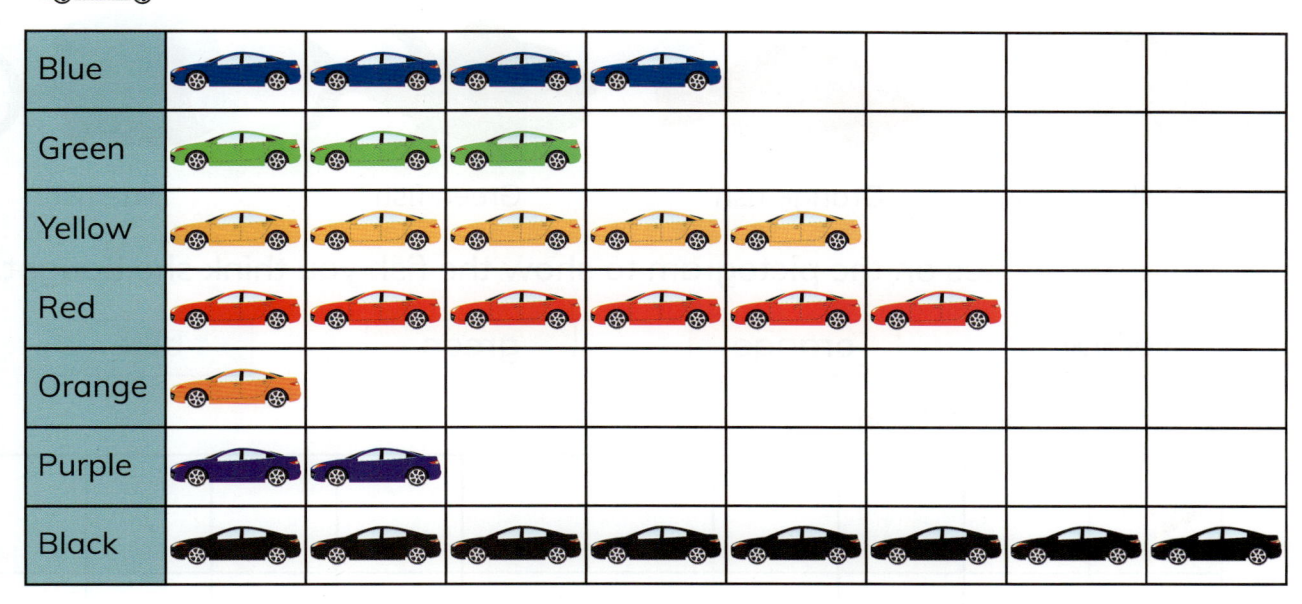

 = 1 car

Blue								
Green								
Yellow								
Red								
Orange								
Purple								
Black								

How many black cars are there? _____

How many red cars are there? _____

How many yellow cars are there? _____

How many more red cars than blue cars are there? _____

How many fewer orange cars than purple cars are there? _____

How many cars are there altogether? _____

137

9 Statistics (2)

2 Work with a partner.

Zara wants to buy some fish. She has enough money for 14 fish.

She can choose from:

Yellow fish   Orange fish   Green fish   Blue fish

Mark the spaces on the pictogram to show the fish you think she bought.

| yellow | orange | green | blue |

1 coloured space = 1 fish

Yellow fish								
Orange fish								
Green fish								
Blue fish								

Write 2 questions about this pictogram for your partner to answer.

1 _____

2 _____

9.2 Pictograms and block graphs

Worked example 2

This block graph shows the favourite colours of children in a class.

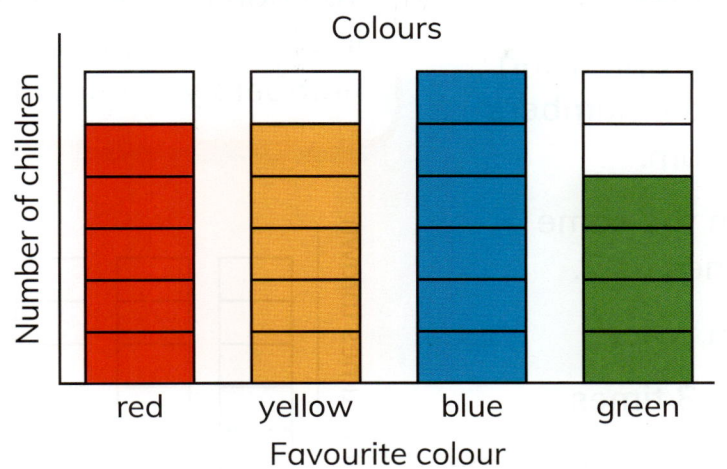

What can you find out using the data in the graph?

We can count the number of shaded blocks. The total number of shaded blocks will tell us how many children there are altogether.

We can also count each colour separately. This shows how many children like each colour best.

Answer: There are 5 red and 5 yellow blocks so that makes 10 children.

There are 4 green and 6 blue blocks so that makes another 10.

That makes 20 children in total.

Blue is the favourite colour because there are more blue blocks.

Green is the least favourite. Only 4 children like green.

9 Statistics (2)

3 This block graph shows the results when a dice is thrown a number of times.

Complete the graph using the data. Use the numbers along the bottom.

4 was thrown the same number of times as 2.

1 was thrown twice.

6 was thrown 3 times.

5 was thrown one more time than 2 and 6.

3 was thrown 7 times.

Write 2 things that you notice.

Tip

You don't have to use the statements in order. Complete the graph for the numbers you know for certain first.

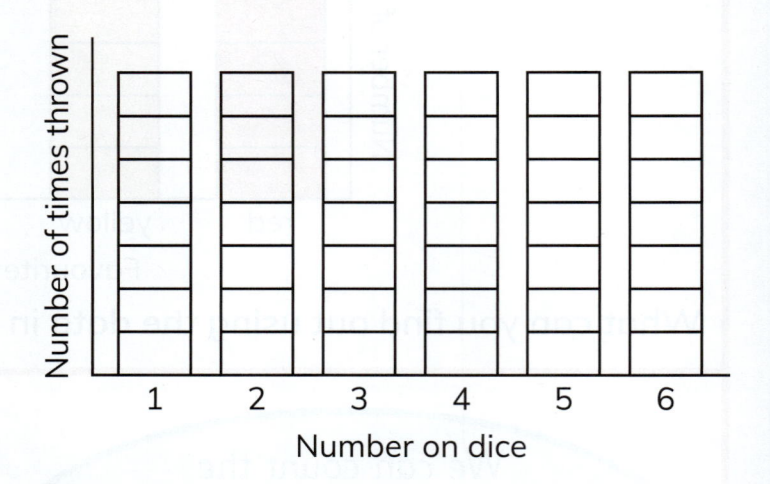

1 _____

2 _____

4 Work as a group of 6.

Ask the question, 'What do you prefer to eat for breakfast: cereal, eggs, a croissant or something else?'

Record the answers and share them with another group of 6.

9.2 Pictograms and block graphs

Use both sets of data to make a pictogram or block graph.
Write the labels and give the graph a title.

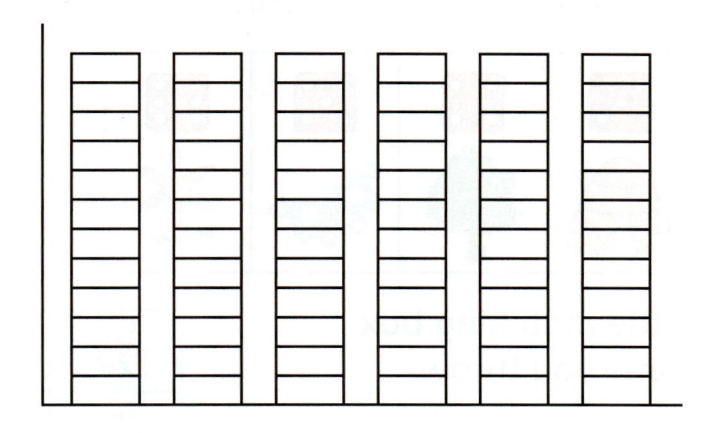

1 ☐ = 1 ☐

Write 2 questions for your partner to answer using the data in the block graph or pictogram.

1 _____

2 _____

9 Statistics (2)

Let's investigate

You will need a dice.

Throw the dice. Use the key to find out which object you have thrown.

Put a tally mark in the matching box in the table every time you throw the dice.

When you have thrown the dice 12 times use the table to complete the matching block graph.

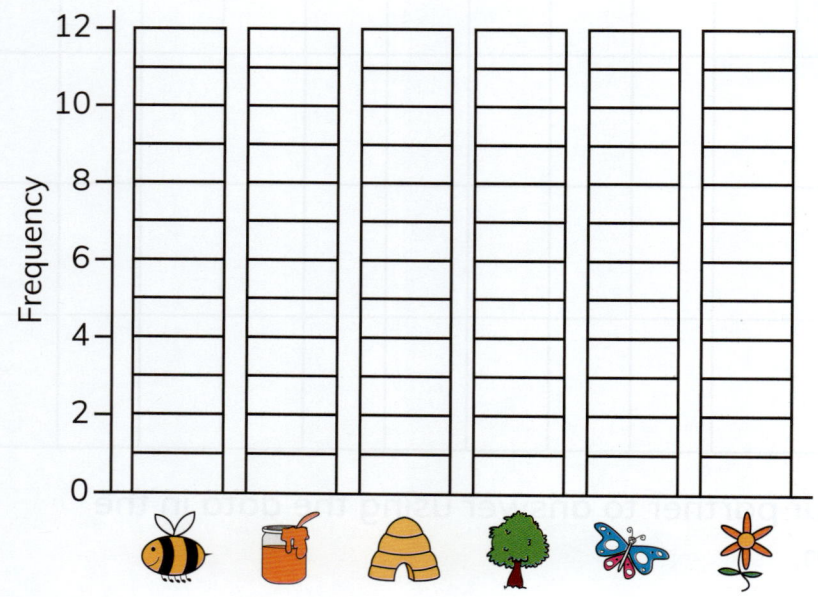

Continued

Complete the sentences.

There are _____ bees. There are _____ jars of honey.

Compare and discuss your block graph with your partner.

What is the same? What is different?

Will the block graphs ever be the same as each other? How many times would we have to play the game?

9 Statistics (2)

5   You are going to plan an investigation about your family.

What do you want to find out?

_____

Write one or more questions you will ask your family.

_____

_____

Record your data.

On a separate piece of paper, draw the data in a graph or diagram.

Tell a partner what you found out.

Ask your teacher for a template to draw on.

Look what I can do!

- I can use data and record it using pictograms and block graphs.
- I can describe the data and discuss results.

9.2 Pictograms and block graphs

Check your progress

1. Use the information in the block graph to complete the pictogram.

A block graph to show the favourite drinks of Class 2

Tea: 5, Milk: 6, Water: 2, Apple: 4, Orange: 1

Favourite drinks pictogram

Tea	🙂						
Milk	🙂	🙂					
Water	🙂						
Apple	🙂	🙂					
Orange							

What is the most popular drink?

How many more people like tea than apple?

2. Complete this Venn diagram using the list of numbers.
   5, 10, 37, 21, 65, 30, 20, 19, 57

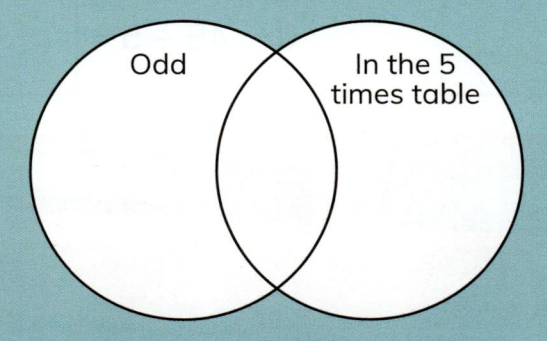

   Odd   In the 5 times table

10 Calculating

Getting started

1. Find the missing answers.

   a) 32
      + 6
      ―――

   b) 67
      − 10
      ―――

   c) 51
      + 10
      ―――

   d) 27
      − 5
      ―――

   e) 76
      + 20
      ―――

   f) 92
      − 40
      ―――

2. Find the missing numbers.

   a) $5 \times 4 =$ ☐

   b) $2 \times 6 =$ ☐

   c) $10 \times 2 =$ ☐

   d) $5 \times 7 =$ ☐

3. Find the missing numbers.

   a) $14 \div 2 =$ ☐

   b) $20 \div 5 =$ ☐

   c) $50 \div 10 =$ ☐

   d) $45 \div 5 =$ ☐

10 Calculating

We add, subtract, multiply and divide to solve all sorts of everyday problems.

When there is an event in the school hall, you can help by getting the correct number of chairs and arranging them in groups or rows for the event.

CRAFT WORKSHOP

We need 45 chairs.

$$\begin{array}{r}21\\+24\\\hline 45\end{array}$$

That's 9 towers of 5. 45 ÷ 5 = 9

Should we have some spare chairs? Another tower of 5?

We could put two tables together and have 10 chairs around each table.

Do we put them in rows of 5 or 10?

10 Calculating

> 10.1 Adding and subtracting two 2-digit numbers

We are going to …

- add two 2-digit numbers
- subtract a 2-digit number from another 2-digit number
- find the difference between two 2-digit numbers.

You will add or subtract numbers almost every day for lots of reasons. This unit helps you to add and subtract tens and ones in the same calculation.

swap   total

Exercise 10.1

1   Add two 2-digit numbers.
    Use some objects on the place value grid to help you calculate.

   a   21 + 47   b   35 + 62   c   54 + 32
       =   =   =

   d   64   e   71   f   46
       + 25   + 16   + 32

10s	1s

10.1 Adding and subtracting two 2-digit numbers

Worked example 1

67 − 32 = ☐

| 10s | 1s |

Cross out 1, 2, 3 of the tens beans.

Cross out 1, 2 of the ones beans.

| 10s | 1s |

> I have crossed out 32.
> I can count what I have not crossed out to find the answer.

67 − 32
= 60 − 30 + 7 − 2
= 30 + 5
= 35

> I split each number into tens and ones.
> 60 − 30 = 30 and 7 − 2 = 5
> 30 + 5 = 35

$$\begin{array}{r} 67 \\ -32 \\ \hline 35 \end{array}$$

> I like to write the calculation out like the place value grid.
> I subtracted the ones then the tens.

149

10 Calculating

2 Solve each number sentence. Show your steps.

a 58 − 35
   =

b 76 − 41
   =

c 67 − 26
   =

3 Complete each subtraction.
Use some objects on the place value grid to help you calculate.

a   89
      − 52

b   56
      − 44

c   78
      − 36

d   67
      − 24

10s	1s

10.1 Adding and subtracting two 2-digit numbers

4 Use the 100 square to help you add or subtract to find the missing numbers.

a   34 + 21 = ☐

b   87 − 43 = ☐

c   69 − 35 = ☐

d   47 + 32 = ☐

Tip

Count on or back in tens and ones to help you find the answers.

1	2	3	4	5	6	7	8	9	10
11	12	13	14	15	16	17	18	19	20
21	22	23	24	25	26	27	28	29	30
31	32	33	34	35	36	37	38	39	40
41	42	43	44	45	46	47	48	49	50
51	52	53	54	55	56	57	58	59	60
61	62	63	64	65	66	67	68	69	70
71	72	73	74	75	76	77	78	79	80
81	82	83	84	85	86	87	88	89	90
91	92	93	94	95	96	97	98	99	100

10 Calculating

5 a Subtract a number in the second cloud from a number in the first cloud.

Write your number sentence.

Which method will you use?

Do this 3 times.

Cloud 1: 79, 56, 68, 87

Cloud 2: 25, 11, 43, 32

b Which calculation will give you the greatest answer?

c Which calculation will give you the smallest answer?

Let's investigate

Choose a number from the grid.

Swap the digits in the number to make a new number.

Add the two numbers together.

For example: 35 + 53 = 88.

What do you notice? Can you explain why this happens? Discuss what you notice with your partner or in a small group.

14	15	16
24	25	26
34	35	36

Arun says that it is easier to record addition and subtraction in columns. What do you think Arun means by 'easier'? Do you agree with Arun?

10.1 Adding and subtracting two 2-digit numbers

6 Sofia made some mistakes when she wrote these number facts.

Tick those that are correct.

Correct any that are not equivalent in value.

24 + 35 = 22 + 36   67 − 23 = 68 − 25

45 + 54 = 44 + 55   56 − 35 = 58 − 37

7 Find the difference between each pair of numbers.

Write the number sentence.
Use a number line or a 100 square to help you.

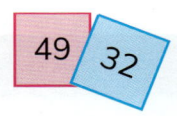

49 32   65 87   54 68

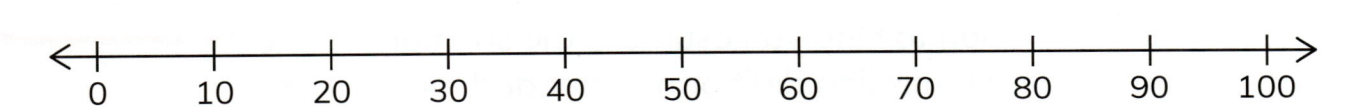

10 Calculating

8 The difference between two numbers is 14.

   If one of the numbers is 45, what could the other number be?

   Did you get the same answer as your partner?
   Is there more than one possible answer?

> **Look what I can do!**
>
> - I can add two 2-digit numbers.
> - I can subtract a 2-digit number from another 2-digit number.
> - I can find the difference between two 2-digit numbers.

> 10.2 Connecting addition and subtraction

> **We are going to …**
>
> - use the connection between addition and subtraction to find the inverse calculation
> - find the addition and subtraction fact family for a set of 3 numbers
> - use rounding to estimate a solution and the inverse calculation to check a solution.

fact family
inverse

Addition and subtraction are closely connected. You can use the inverse calculation to help you estimate the solution, check the calculation, find a missing digit or number and much more.

10.2 Connecting addition and subtraction

Exercise 10.2

1 Find the inverse calculations.

Calculation	Inverse
4 + 6 = 10	
12 + 7 = 19	
21 + 26 = 47	
10 − 8 = 2	
17 − 6 = 11	
39 − 16 = 23	

2 Find the inverse calculation to check each calculation.

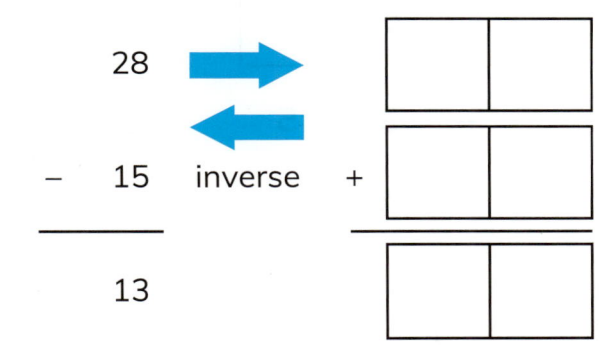

```
    19              inverse         28              inverse
  − 4      →      +               − 15     →      +
  ___      ←      ___             ___      ←      ___
   15                              13
```

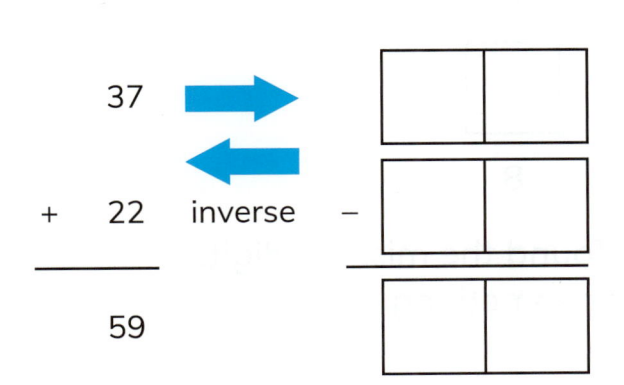

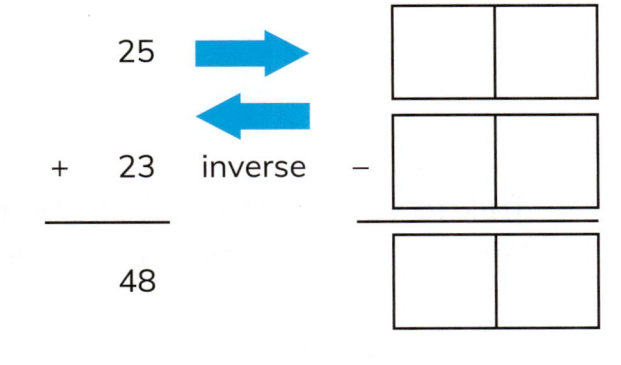

```
    37              inverse         25              inverse
  + 22     →      −               + 23     →      −
  ___      ←      ___             ___      ←      ___
   59                              48
```

10 Calculating

3 Write 6 number bonds for 10. Write the inverse calculation for each number bond for 10.

> Arun says to find the inverse calculation, all you need to do is read the calculation from the end to the beginning. Do you agree with Arun?

4 Find the missing digit in each calculation.

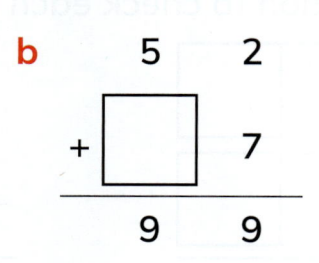

a)
```
   7 ☐
 − 3 5
 ─────
   4 1
```

b)
```
   5 2
 + ☐ 7
 ─────
   9 9
```

c)
```
   ☐ 3
 − 4 2
 ─────
   2 1
```

d)
```
   4 5
 + 3 ☐
 ─────
   7 8
```

Talk to your partner about how you found the missing digit. Did you use the inverse calculation or something else?

10.2 Connecting addition and subtraction

5 Write the fact family for this part whole representation.

___ + ___ = ___   ___ = ___ + ___

___ + ___ = ___   ___ = ___ + ___

___ − ___ = ___   ___ = ___ − ___

___ − ___ = ___   ___ = ___ − ___

6 Complete each fact family house.

a 3 / 6 9

___ + ___ = ___

___ = ___ + ___

___ + ___ = ___

___ = ___ + ___

___ − ___ = ___

___ = ___ − ___

___ − ___ = ___

___ = ___ − ___

b 17 / 8 9

___ + ___ = ___

___ = ___ + ___

___ + ___ = ___

___ = ___ + ___

___ − ___ = ___

___ = ___ − ___

___ − ___ = ___

___ = ___ − ___

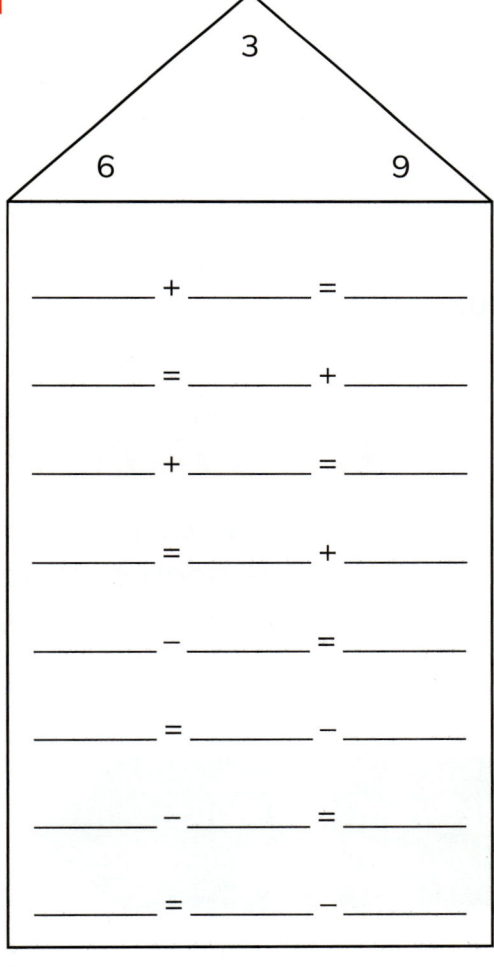

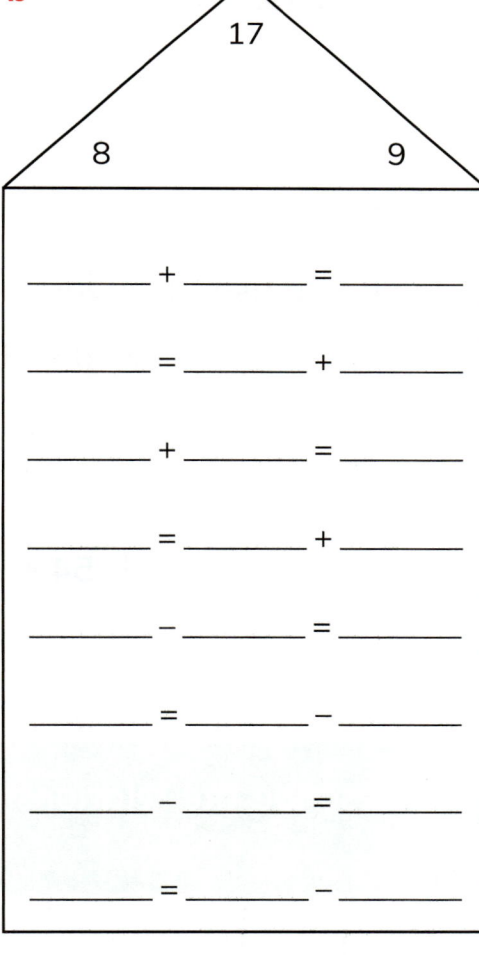

10 Calculating

Let's investigate

The wind has blown the roof away from a fact family house! Here is part of the roof.

What could the fact family be?
Is there more than one answer?

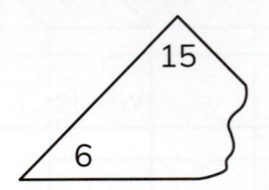

> Share your results with your partner.
> Are your results the same?
> Convince each other that you have found all the solutions.

7 The number sentence 40 + 30 = 70 shows two complements of 70. Write the 4 subtraction calculations using the same set of three numbers.

8 Estimate, solve and use the inverse calculation to check.

   a   42 + 37   b   89 − 62

   c   77 − 34   d   54 + 33

Tip

Round each number to the nearest 10 to estimate your answer.

> How could you describe the relationship between addition and subtraction?

158

10.3 Multiplication

Look what I can do!

- I can use the connection between addition and subtraction to find the inverse calculation.
- I can find the addition and subtraction fact family for a set of 3 numbers.
- I can use rounding to estimate a solution and the inverse calculation to check a solution.

> 10.3 Multiplication

We are going to ...

- find connections between the multiplication tables (1×, 2×, 5× and 10×)
- connect multiplying by 2 with doubling
- recognise that number facts on either side of the = sign have the same value.

Multiplication tables are lists of facts about one number. They are very useful to know when working with equal groups in any situation.

product

You can use one multiplication fact to find another, doubling any fact about 5× to find a 10× fact.

159

10 Calculating

Exercise 10.3

1. Write the multiplication sentences.
   The first one has been done for you.

   Double: 5 × 3 = 15 → __10 × 3 = 30__

   Half of: 10 × 4 = 40 → _____

   Double: 5 × 8 = 40 → _____

   Half of: 10 × 7 = 70 → _____

2. Marcus used 8 hands to make two different multiplication facts from the multiplication table for 5.
   What could those facts be?

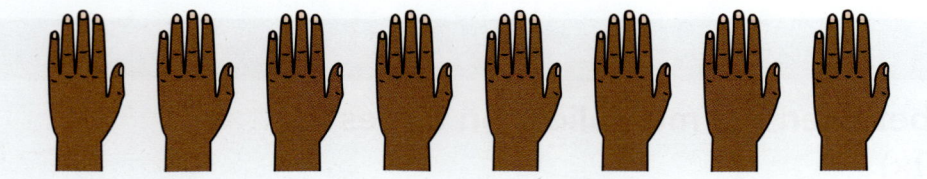

   Sofia also used 8 hands, but she made two different multiplication facts for the multiplication table for 10.
   What could those facts be?

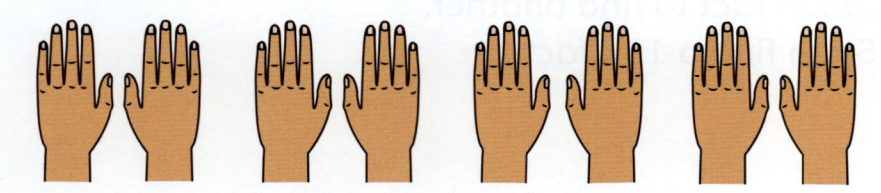

160

10.3 Multiplication

3   Use the connection between doubling and multiplying by 2 to find the missing facts.

Multiplying by 2	Doubling
	2 + 2 = 4
5 × 2 = 10	
	1 + 1 = 2
10 × 2 = 20	

4   The equal product machine makes equivalent multiplication calculations. What calculation might come out of the machine?

5 × 4 = 20

2 × 3 = 6

10 × 3 = 30

Write your three equivalent facts.

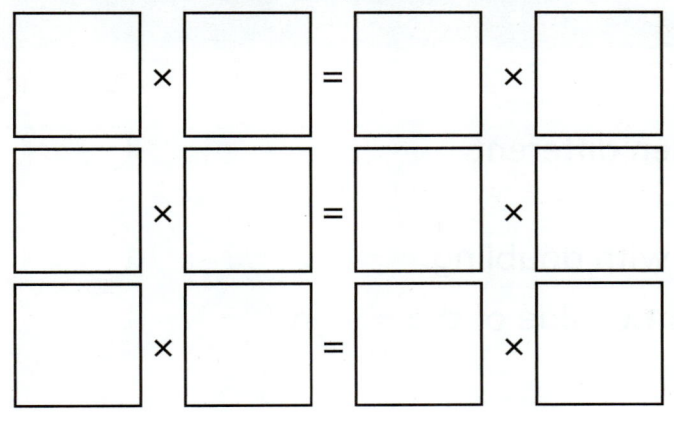

☐ × ☐ = ☐ × ☐

☐ × ☐ = ☐ × ☐

☐ × ☐ = ☐ × ☐

161

10 Calculating

5 The teacher pointed to this place on the counting stick.
   Which multiplication facts could this represent?

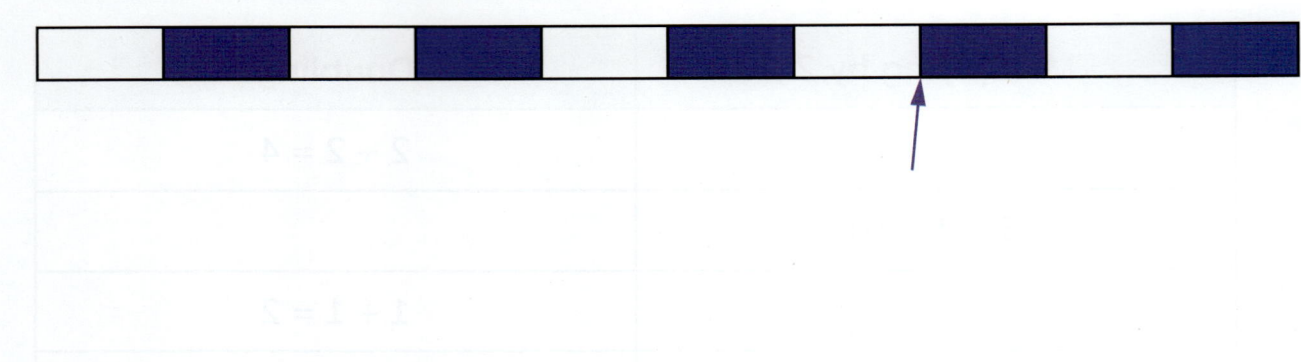

6 Which pair of equivalent multiplication facts do these cubes represent?

> **Let's investigate**
>
> The products in some multiplication tables have the pattern odd, even, odd, even. Others have only even products. Why is that?
>
> Discuss your answers with a partner.

Look what I can do!

- I can make connections between different multiplication tables.
- I can connect multiplying by 2 with doubling.
- I know that number facts on either side of the = sign have the same value.

10.4 Division

> **We are going to ...**
> - build division tables from multiplication tables
> - connect number facts with the same value
> - connect halving with dividing by 2 and finding a quarter with dividing by 4.

Division is all about equal groups, just like multiplication.

You can use a multiplication fact to find a division fact. Finding a half or a quarter is the same as dividing by 2 and 4.

You don't have to learn everything in mathematics, there are so many connections to use.

quotient

Exercise 10.4

1 Complete the multiplication table for 5. Use it to write the division facts for 5.

   $5 \times 1 = 5$　　　　　　　　　　　　$5 \div 5 = 1$

   $5 \times 2 = 10$　　　　　　　　　　　 _____

   $5 \times 3 = $ _____　　　 _____

   $5 \times 4 = $ _____　　　 _____

   _____　　　 _____

   _____　　　 _____

   _____　　　 _____

   _____　　　 _____

10 Calculating

2 Write the inverse division fact for each multiplication fact.

a $2 \times 6 = 12 \rightarrow$ _____

b $1 \times 8 = 8 \rightarrow$ _____

c $10 \times 4 = 40 \rightarrow$ _____

d $5 \times 3 = 15 \rightarrow$ _____

3 When a product and a quotient have the same value, the facts are equal in value.

You can join them using the equals sign, for example, $6 \times 1 = 12 \div 2$.

Write a multiplication or division fact with the same value as the given fact. Write a multiplication fact if the given fact is a division, and a division fact if the given fact is a multiplication.

a $2 \times 4 =$ _____

b $1 \times 3 =$ _____

c $14 \div 2 =$ _____

d $30 \div 5 =$ _____

4 Is each division fact the equivalent to finding $\frac{1}{2}$ or $\frac{1}{4}$?

Division fact	Equivalent to finding $\frac{1}{2}$ or $\frac{1}{4}$?
$8 \div 2 = 4$	
$12 \div 4 = 3$	
$20 \div 4 = 5$	
$10 \div 2 = 5$	

10.4 Division

> **Let's investigate**
>
> Grandma is buying Zara and her 3 brothers some chocolate.
> They can each have a small bar like this 
>
> or a larger bar like this one to share. 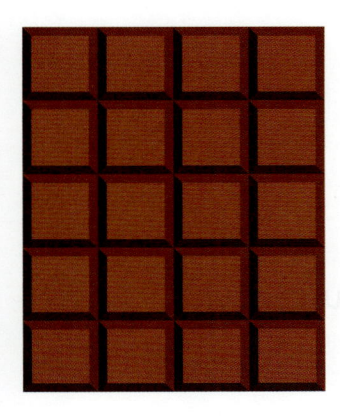
>
> Which bar should they choose? Why?
>
> Work with a partner.
> Write some number sentences to show how you found your answer.

5   Write some division facts to connect with this multiplication fact.

I know that 10 × 2 = 20 so I also know that . . .

10 Calculating

6 Write 4 multiplication, division or fraction facts about this array.

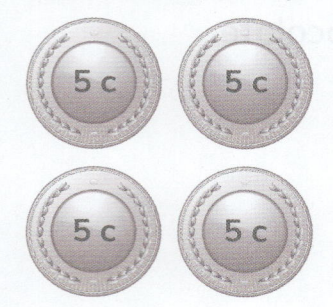

7 Make up a question like question 6 using your own currency.

Swap questions with a friend and answer it.

Ask your friend to check that you were correct.

Look what I can do!
• I can build division tables from multiplication tables.
• I can connect number facts with the same value.
• I can connect halving with dividing by 2 and finding a quarter with dividing by 4.

10.4 Division

Check your progress

1 Complete these additions and subtractions.

    a   43   b   55   c   89   d   76
       + 35   + 42   − 46   − 41

2 The three numbers 24, 35 and 59 make a fact family.
   Write the 8 calculations in the fact family.

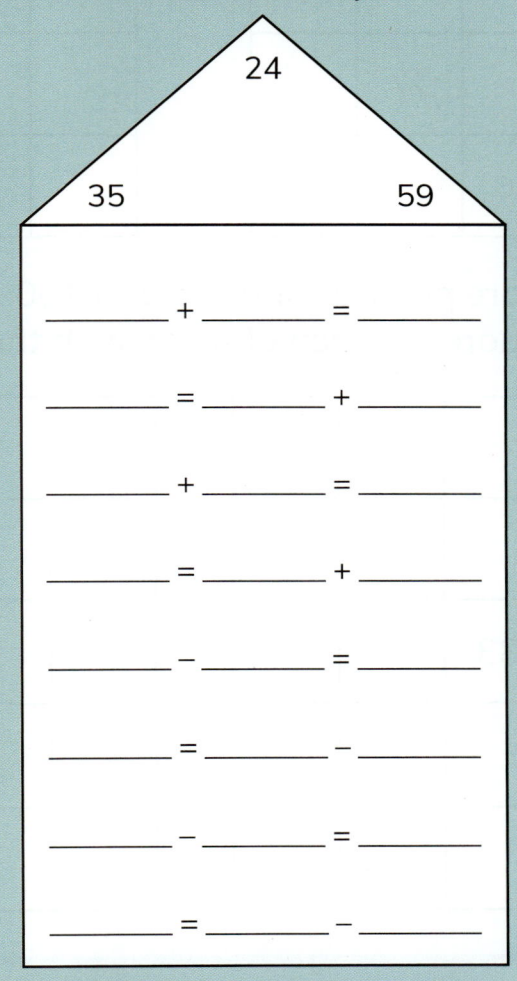

                   24

     35   59

_____ + _____ = _____

_____ = _____ + _____

_____ + _____ = _____

_____ = _____ + _____

_____ − _____ = _____

_____ = _____ − _____

_____ − _____ = _____

_____ = _____ − _____

3 Complete the equivalent calculations.

   a   ☐ × ☐ = ☐ ÷ ☐ = $\frac{1}{2}$ of 12.

   b $\frac{1}{4}$ of 12 = ☐ × ☐ = ☐ ÷ ☐ = ☐ − ☐.

Project 5

100 square

1 Here are two pictures of parts of a 100 square. Fill in the empty squares in each of these with the correct numbers.

		18
	27	
36		

23		
	34	
		45

2 Here are two more pictures of parts of a 100 square. Fill in all of the empty squares in each of these with the correct numbers.

				15
		33		
51				

52				
			74	
				96

Project 5: 100 square

Continued

3 Now we are looking at some diagonal lines of numbers taken from a 100 square. What does the question mark represent in each of these diagonal lines?

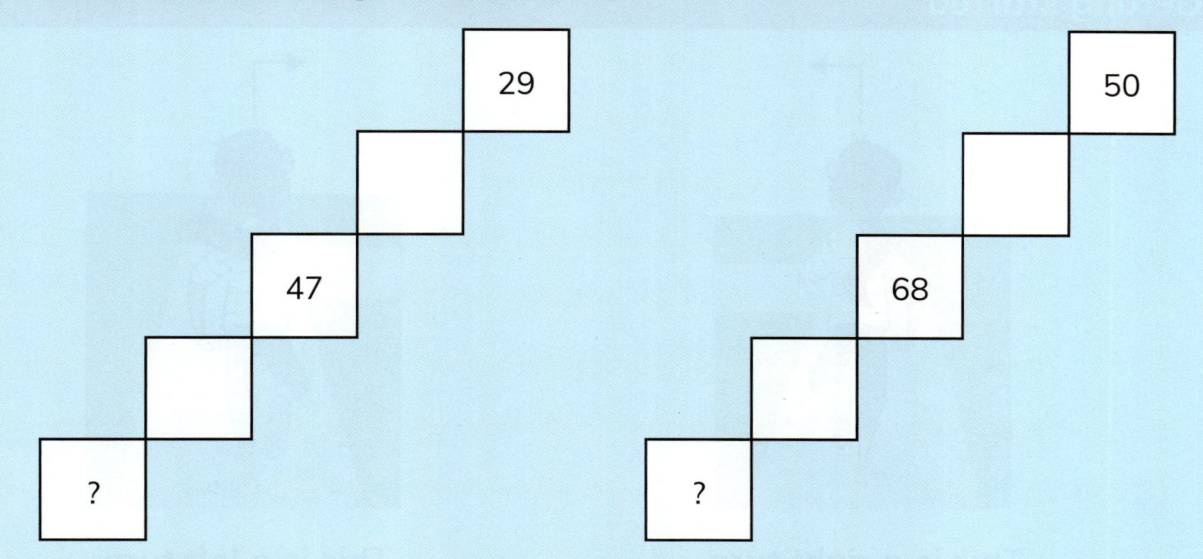

[Left diagonal: 29 at top, 47 in middle, ? at bottom]

[Right diagonal: 50 at top, 68 in middle, ? at bottom]

4 This next grid has something special! Look at the number in the top right-hand corner and compare it to the number in the bottom left-hand corner. What do you notice?

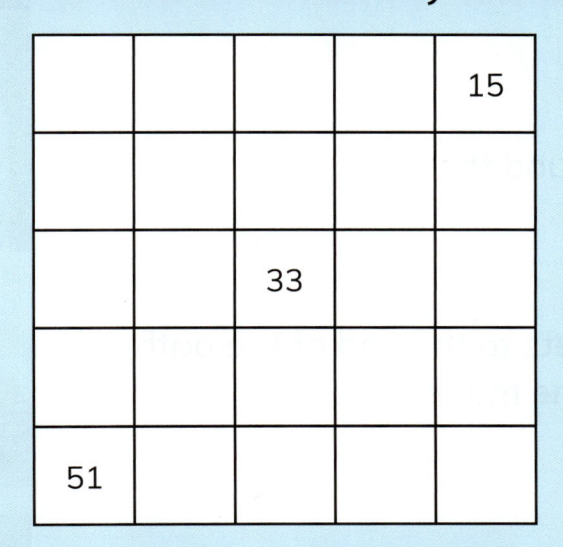

[5×5 grid with 15 in top right, 33 in centre, 51 in bottom left]

Talk to your partner about how you could find more grids in the 100 square where the same thing happens.
How many can you find?

11 Geometry (2)

Getting started

This is a right turn.

This is a left turn.

1. When the girl gets to the end of the path, what turn will she make?

   Left or right?

   Draw a ring around the correct answer.

2. When the girl gets to the end of the path, what turn will she make?

   Left or right?

   Draw a ring around the correct answer.

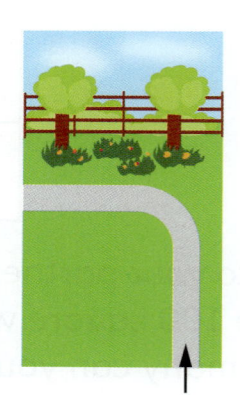

11 Geometry (2)

This unit will teach you about turns and angles.

These are quarter turns:

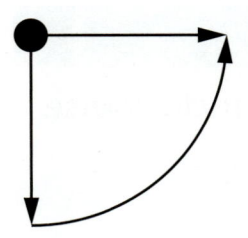

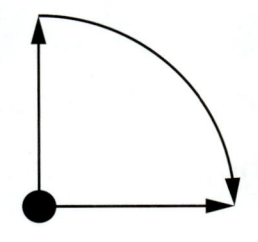

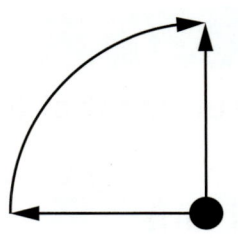

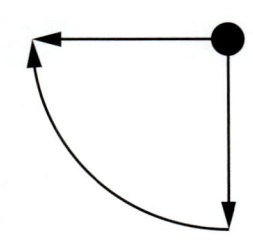

These are half turns:

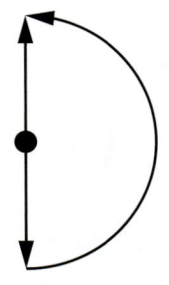

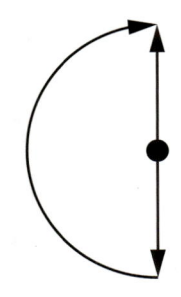

This is a full turn:

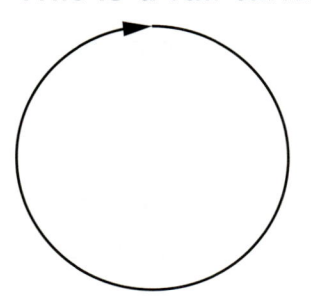

An angle is the space between two lines:

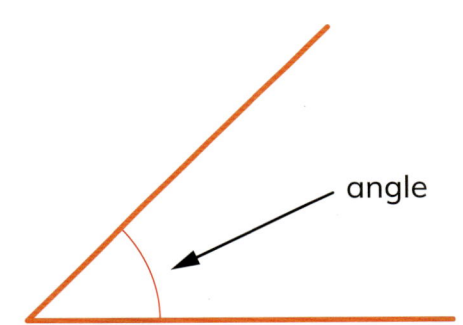

angle

All circles have a centre:

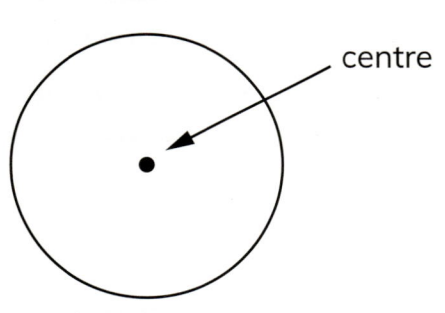

centre

You will also learn about circles.

171

11 Geometry (2)

> 11.1 Angles and turns

We are going to ...

- use angles as a measurement of turn both clockwise and anticlockwise
- predict and check how many times a shape looks the same as it completes a full turn.

There are angles everywhere! Look at this clock. The minute hand and hour hand make an angle where they meet.

Clock hands also turn. The direction that they move is called clockwise. Anticlockwise is the opposite direction.

Anticlockwise

Clockwise

> angle   anticlockwise   clockwise   full turn
> half turn   quarter turn   right angle   turn

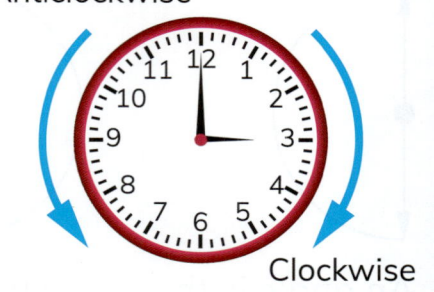

Exercise 11.1

Worked example 1

Which way should the child turn so she can see the cube?

I think she should turn anticlockwise.

I think she should turn clockwise.

Answer: She could turn both ways to see the cube.

172

11.1 Angles and turns

1 a   The tortoise always looks in the direction he is walking.

He travels along the green path.

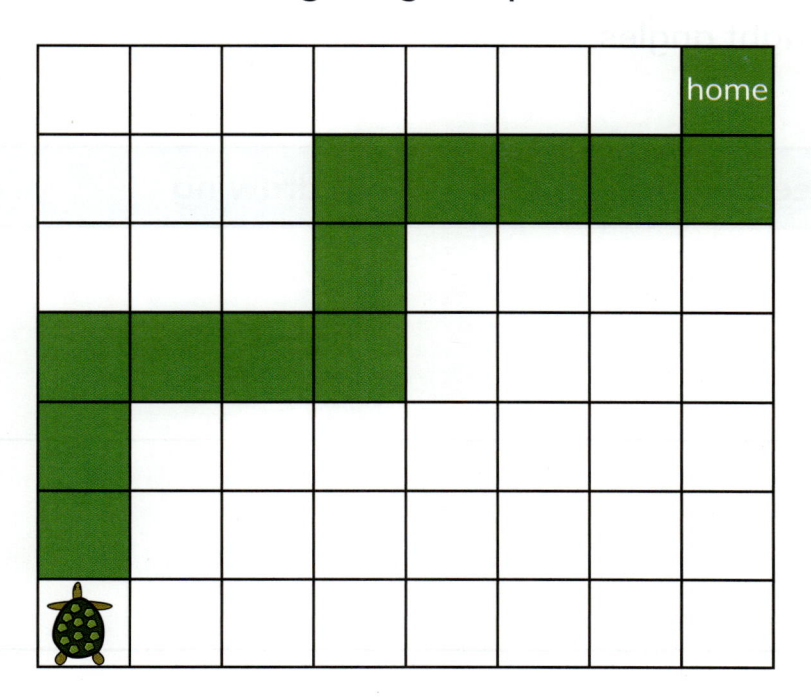

How many times did he turn a quarter turn clockwise? _____

How many times did he turn a quarter turn anticlockwise? _____

How many right angle turns did he make altogether? _____

b   Colour a different path to get the tortoise home.

How many quarter turns clockwise? _____

How many quarter turns anticlockwise? _____

How many right angle turns did he make altogether? _____

173

11 Geometry (2)

2. Work with a partner.

   Look around you and make a list of six angles that you can see.

   Try to find at least 3 right angles.

   Draw them.

What can you see?	Your drawing

11.1 Angles and turns

3   Turn the shapes a half turn clockwise and draw them.

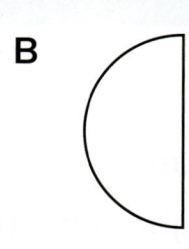

A

B

Would each shape fit exactly on top of its drawing?

A _____

B _____

Predict and then check how many half turns would be needed to make the shapes look identical.

A _____

B _____

4   Turn the shapes a quarter turn anticlockwise and draw them.

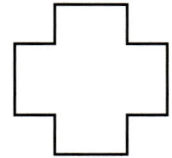

A

B

Would they fit exactly on top of each other?

A _____

B _____

Predict and then check how many quarter turns would be needed to make the shapes look identical.

A _____

B _____

11 Geometry (2)

Let's investigate

You have 2 sticks:

1 red _____   1 blue _____

Draw how you can make one right angle using sticks.

Draw how you can make two right angles using 2 sticks.

Talk to your partner. Can you make three and four right angles with 2 sticks?

If you can, draw them, if you can't, write why not.

Activity adapted from NRICH Right Angle Challenge.

Look what I can do!

- I can use angles as a measurement of turn both clockwise and anticlockwise.
- I can predict and check how many times a shape looks the same as it completes a full turn.

> 11.2 Circles

We are going to ...
- find the centre of a circle by folding
- use folded circles to find angles and turns.

A circle is a round 2D shape.

All points on the edge of the circle are the same distance to the centre.

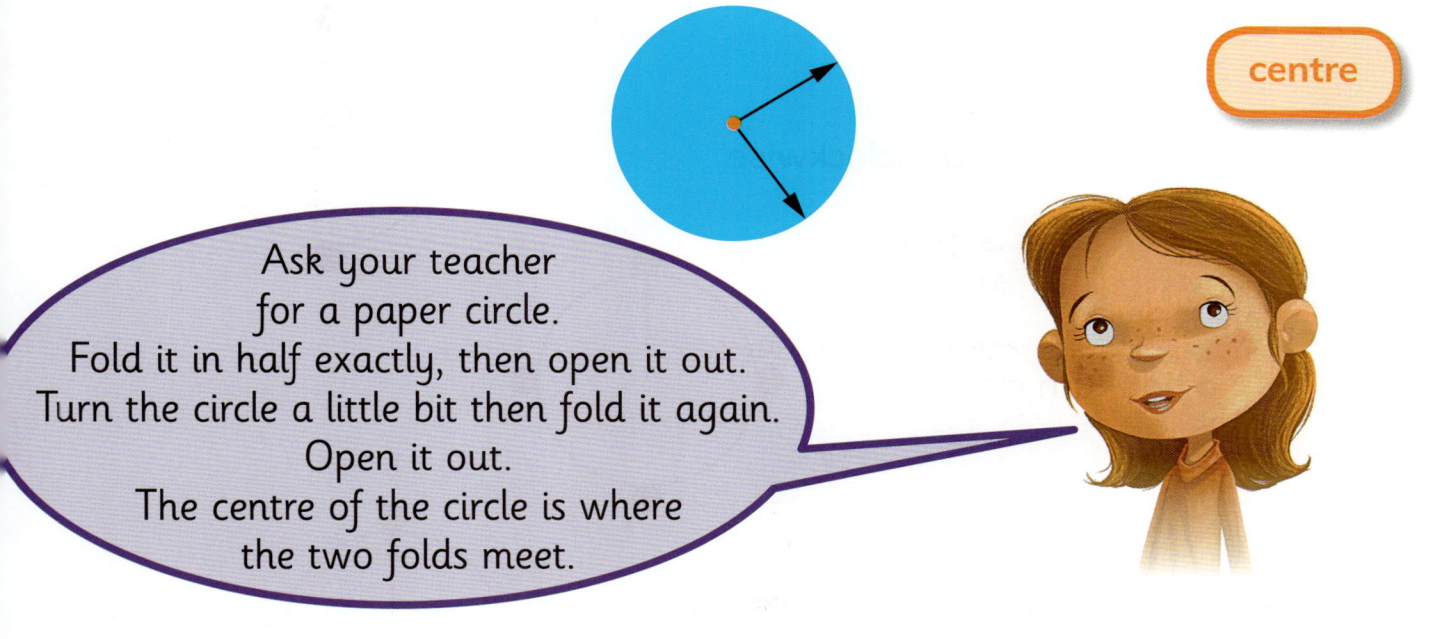

centre

> Ask your teacher for a paper circle.
> Fold it in half exactly, then open it out.
> Turn the circle a little bit then fold it again.
> Open it out.
> The centre of the circle is where the two folds meet.

Any line that is drawn from one edge to the other and through the centre of the circle makes a line of symmetry.

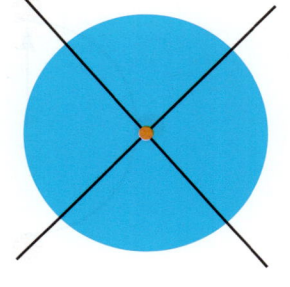

Circles are all over the world: in art, nature, buildings, and in our homes.

11 Geometry (2)

Exercise 11.2

1. An angle is the amount of turn between two lines that meet each other.

   Use your folded paper circle to draw the lines that show:

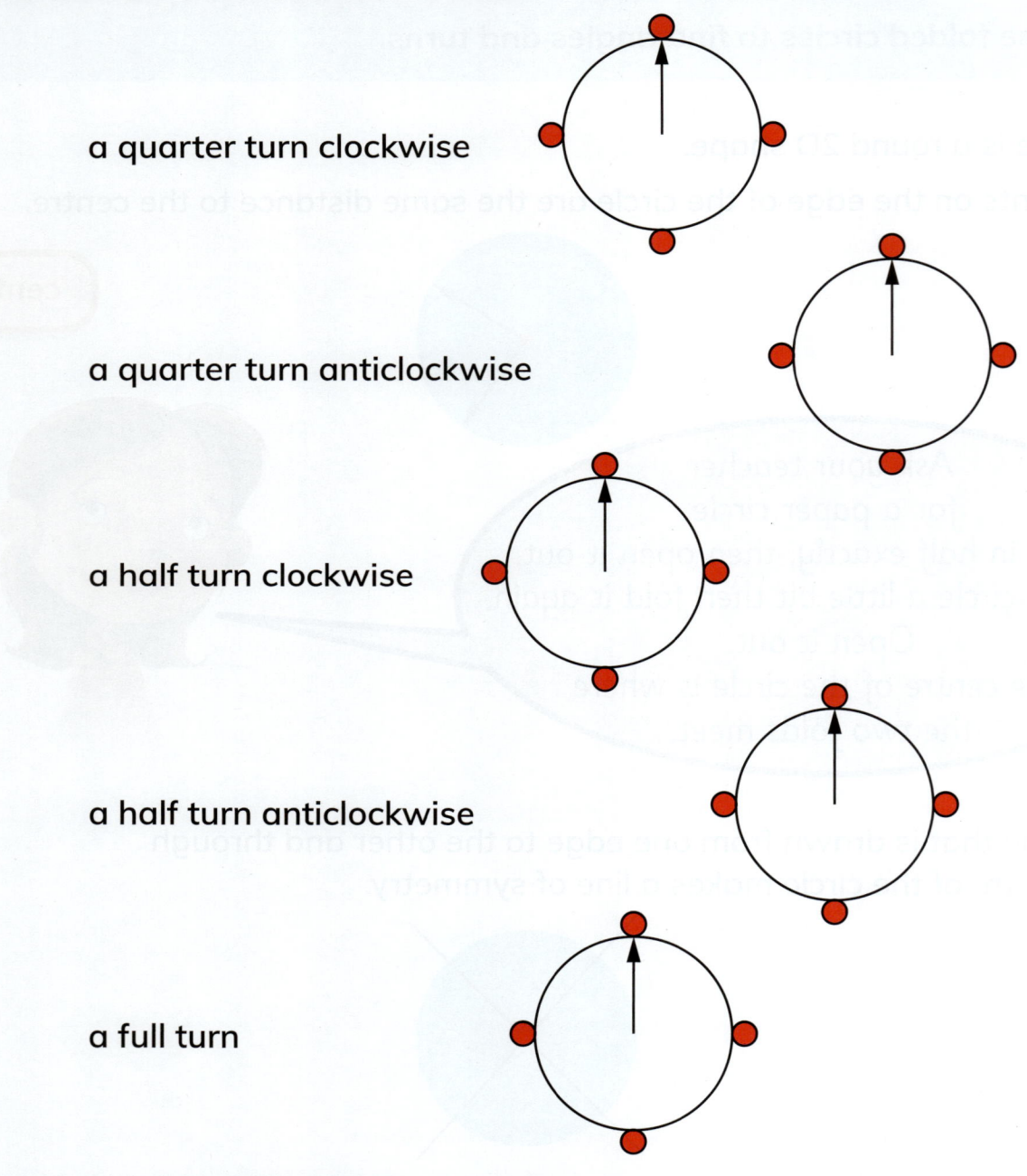

   a quarter turn clockwise

   a quarter turn anticlockwise

   a half turn clockwise

   a half turn anticlockwise

   a full turn

   How many of your lines made a right angle at the centre of the circle?

11.2 Circles

2 Use your folded paper circles to help you draw the
   lines that show:

   a   2 right angles   b   a half turn

   c   a quarter turn anticlockwise

Let's investigate

Next time you see a bike, look at the
wheels. As they turn, the shape of
the wheels stays the same.

Work with your partner.

Look at these 2 wheels.

What is the same about them? What is different?

Draw 2 different car wheels.

Write 2 things that are the same.

Write 2 things that are different.

11 Geometry (2)

Look what I can do!

- I can find the centre of a circle by folding.
- I can use the folded circles to find angles and turns.

Check your progress

1 Which of these dots show the centre of the circle?

2 Look at what your partner is wearing.
   Draw 2 things that show angles.

3 Draw where the red spot will be   after

   a quarter turn anticlockwise

   a quarter turn clockwise

11.2 Circles

Continued

4   How many times does each spinning toy look the same during a full turn?

12 Telling the time

Getting started

1 Count in fives to find the answers.

   5 × 1 = ☐   5 × 5 = ☐   5 × 9 = ☐

   5 × 2 = ☐   5 × 6 = ☐   5 × 10 = ☐

   5 × 3 = ☐   5 × 7 = ☐   5 × 11 = ☐

   5 × 4 = ☐   5 × 8 = ☐   5 × 12 = ☐

2 Draw a line to match the times that are the same.

   half past 11

   5 o'clock

   half past 3

   half past 8

12 Telling the time

In this unit, you will find out how analogue and digital clocks show the time in different ways.

"We're early!"

"Our train leaves at 20 past 10."

"I wonder what 10:20 will look like on my watch …"

12 Telling the time

> 12.1 Telling the time

> **We are going to …**
> - read and record the time to 5 minutes on analogue and digital clocks
> - find out what is meant by quarter past and quarter to the hour.

You need to be able to read and record the time so that you can be in the correct place at the correct time.

Telling the time means you can meet your friends, catch a train or a bus, go to the cinema and so much more.

> analogue clock
> digital clock
> quarter past
> quarter to

Exercise 12.1

1 How many minutes are in 1 hour? ☐ minutes

> Zara wrote 12 as the answer to question 1. How could you explain the correct answer?

2 How many minutes are in half an hour? ☐ minutes

12.1 Telling the time

Worked example 1

Make the analogue and digital clocks show 20 minutes to 5.

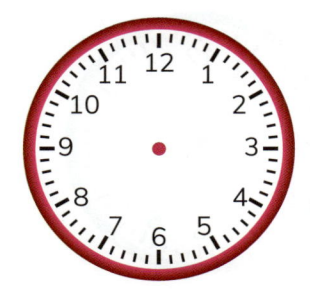

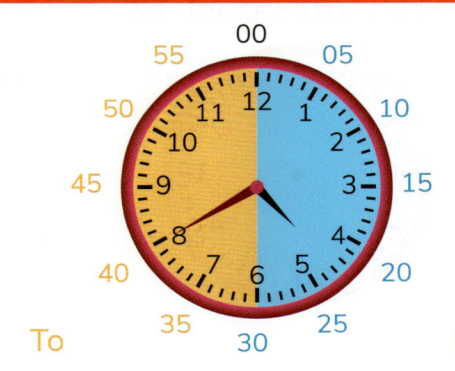

1. Draw in the minute hand on the analogue clock.

   20 minutes until the next hour is the same as 40 minutes past the hour. The minute hand must be at the 8.

2. Now draw the hour hand on the analogue clock.

   The hour hand must be more than halfway beyond 4 but not as far as 5.

3. Write the time in numbers on the digital clock.

   20 to is the same as 40 past, so the digital time is 4:40.

185

12 Telling the time

3 Make the analogue and digital clocks show the correct time.

20 minutes past 10	5 minutes past 7
30 minutes past 11	15 minutes past 12
10 minutes past 8	25 minutes past 9

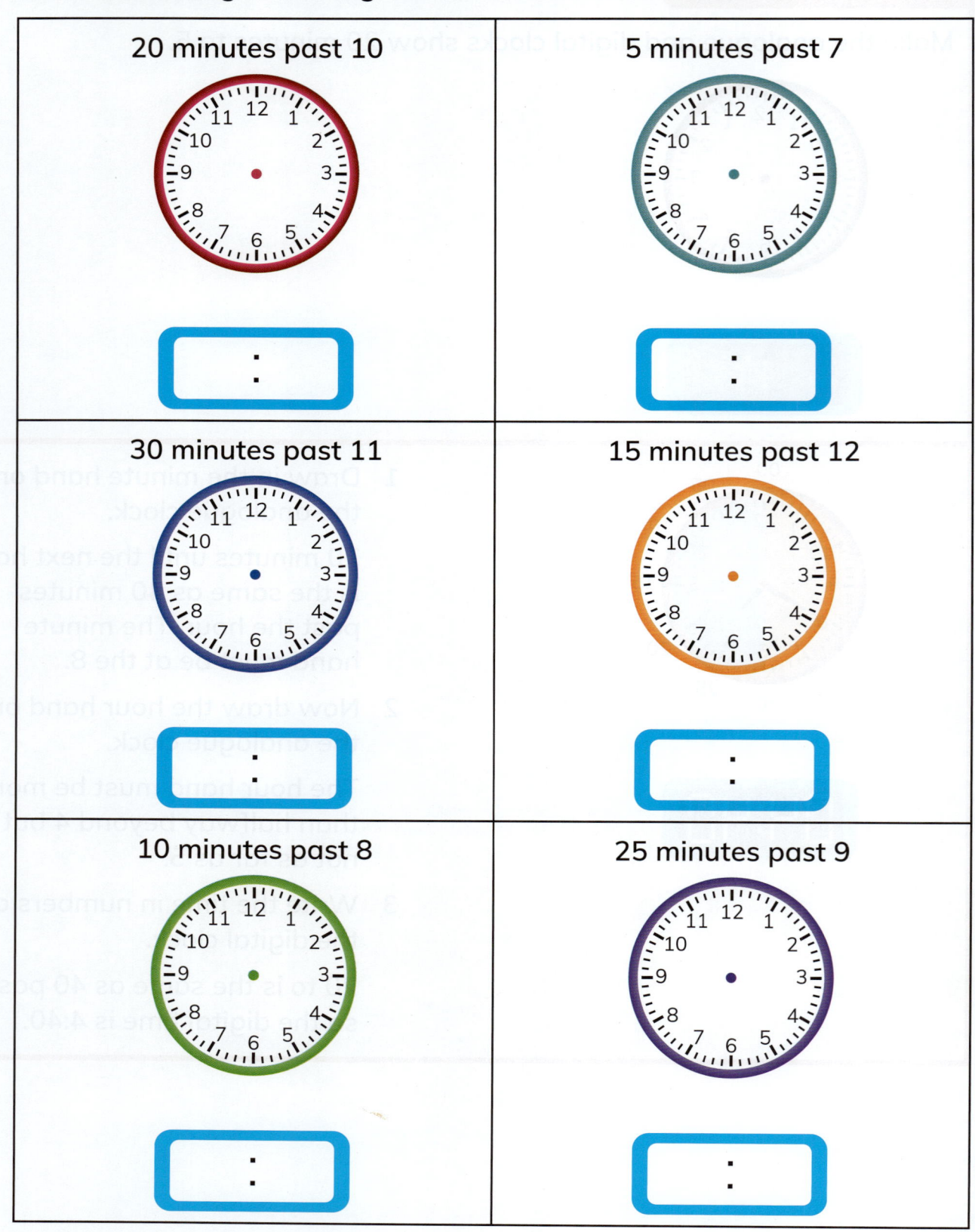

12.1 Telling the time

4 Make the analogue and digital clocks show the correct time.

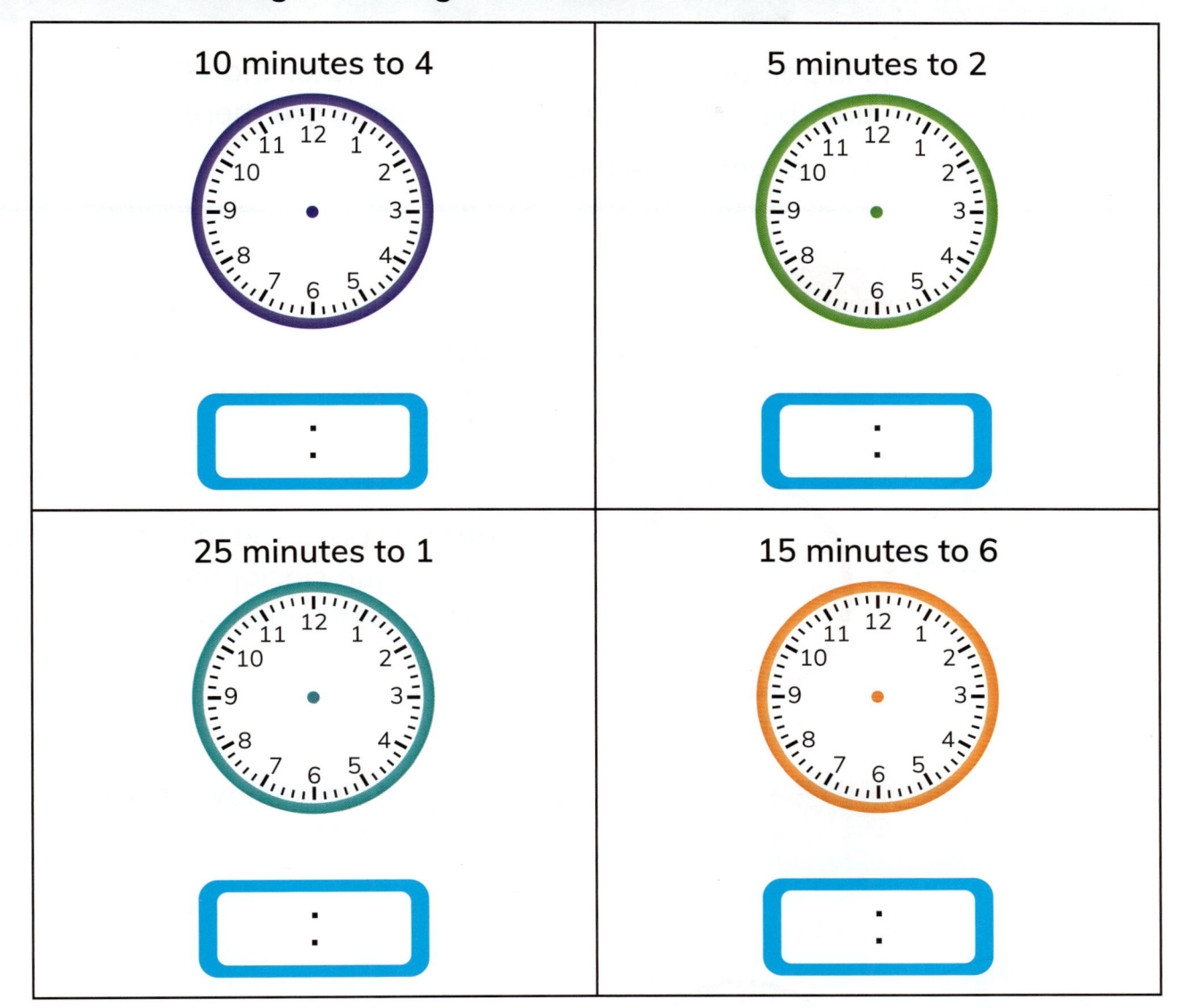

10 minutes to 4

5 minutes to 2

25 minutes to 1

15 minutes to 6

When you say a time, you often use 'past' or 'to'. What do 'past' and 'to' mean?

12 Telling the time

> **Let's investigate**
>
> The minute hand is pointing to an odd number greater than 6. What could the time be? How many different times are there?
>
> Discuss your answers with a partner.

Worked example 2

What is the difference between quarter past and quarter to the hour?

Quarter past

quarter — quarter past

At quarter past, the minute hand on the analogue clock points to the 3. It is 15 minutes past the hour.

12:15

The digital clock shows the hour number and 15 minutes.

Quarter to

three-quarters — quarter to

At quarter to, the minute hand on the analogue clock points to the 9. It is 45 minutes past the hour and 15 minutes to the next hour.

12:45

The digital clock shows the hour number and 45 minutes.

12.1 Telling the time

5 Complete the clocks and write the time in words.

Analogue clock	Time in words	Digital clock
		:
		:
		10:45
		04:15

189

12 Telling the time

6 Complete the clocks.
Draw a ring around the correct time of day.

Quarter to 5		Morning
		Afternoon
_ _ : _ _		Evening

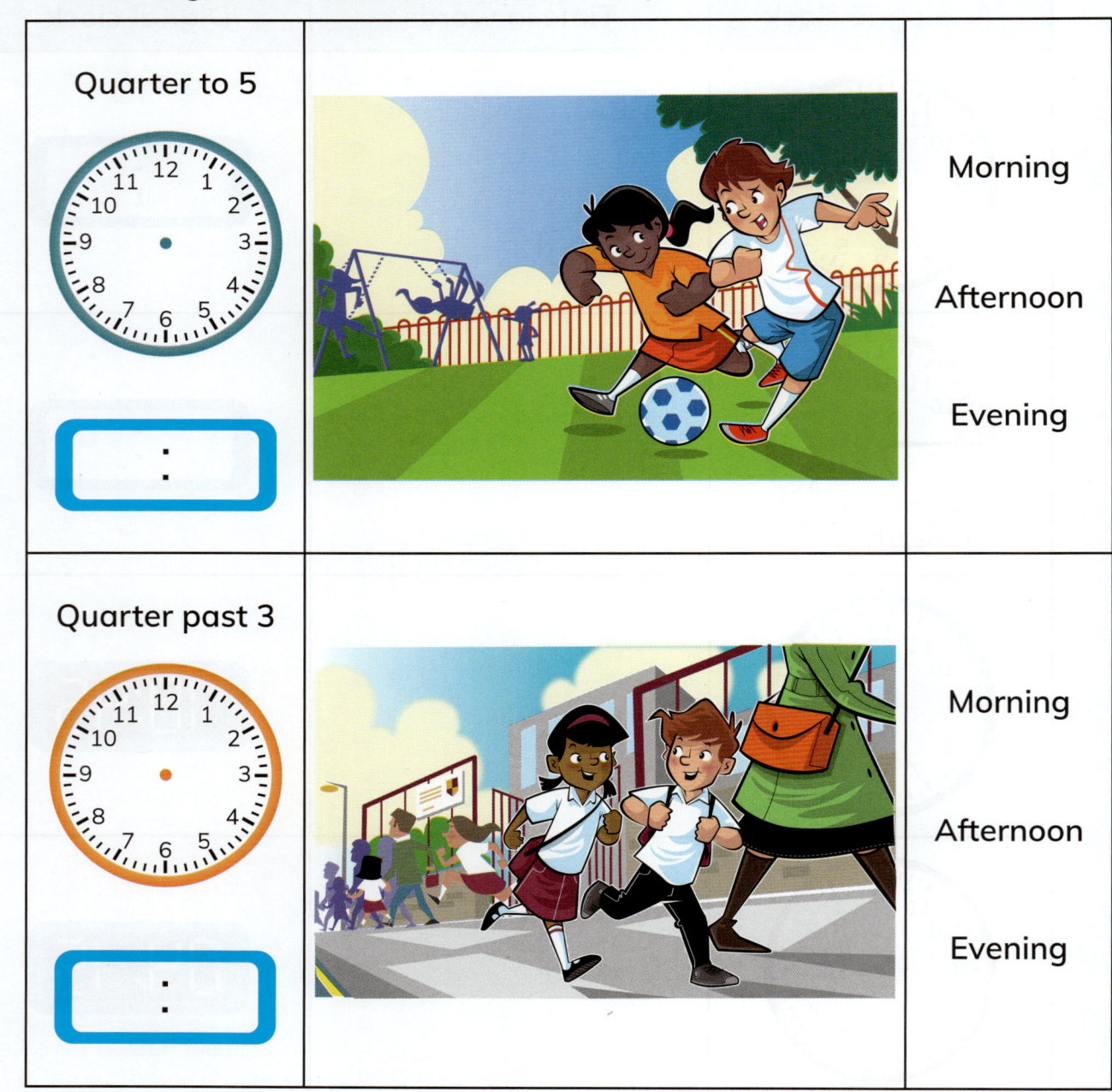

Quarter past 3		Morning
		Afternoon
_ _ : _ _		Evening

190

12.1 Telling the time

Quarter to 8		Morning
		Afternoon
☐ : ☐		Evening
Quarter past 8		Morning
		Afternoon
☐ : ☐		Evening

Look what I can do!

- I can read and record the time to 5 minutes on analogue and digital clocks.
- I can read and record quarter past and quarter to the hour on analogue and digital clocks.

12 Telling the time

Check your progress

1 Which clocks show quarter to 11?

2 Show each time on the analogue and digital clocks.

| 25 minutes past 3 | 20 minutes to 12 | 5 minutes to 6 | Quarter past 9 |

3 Sofia drew a picture of herself brushing her teeth at 10 minutes past 8.
   She forgot to write morning, afternoon or evening on her picture.
   Which times of the day could she have written?

13 ▶ Measures (2)

Getting started

The mass of a paper clip is **half** the mass of a block.

The mass of a block is **double** the mass of a paper clip.

Draw blocks to balance the paper clips on each scale.

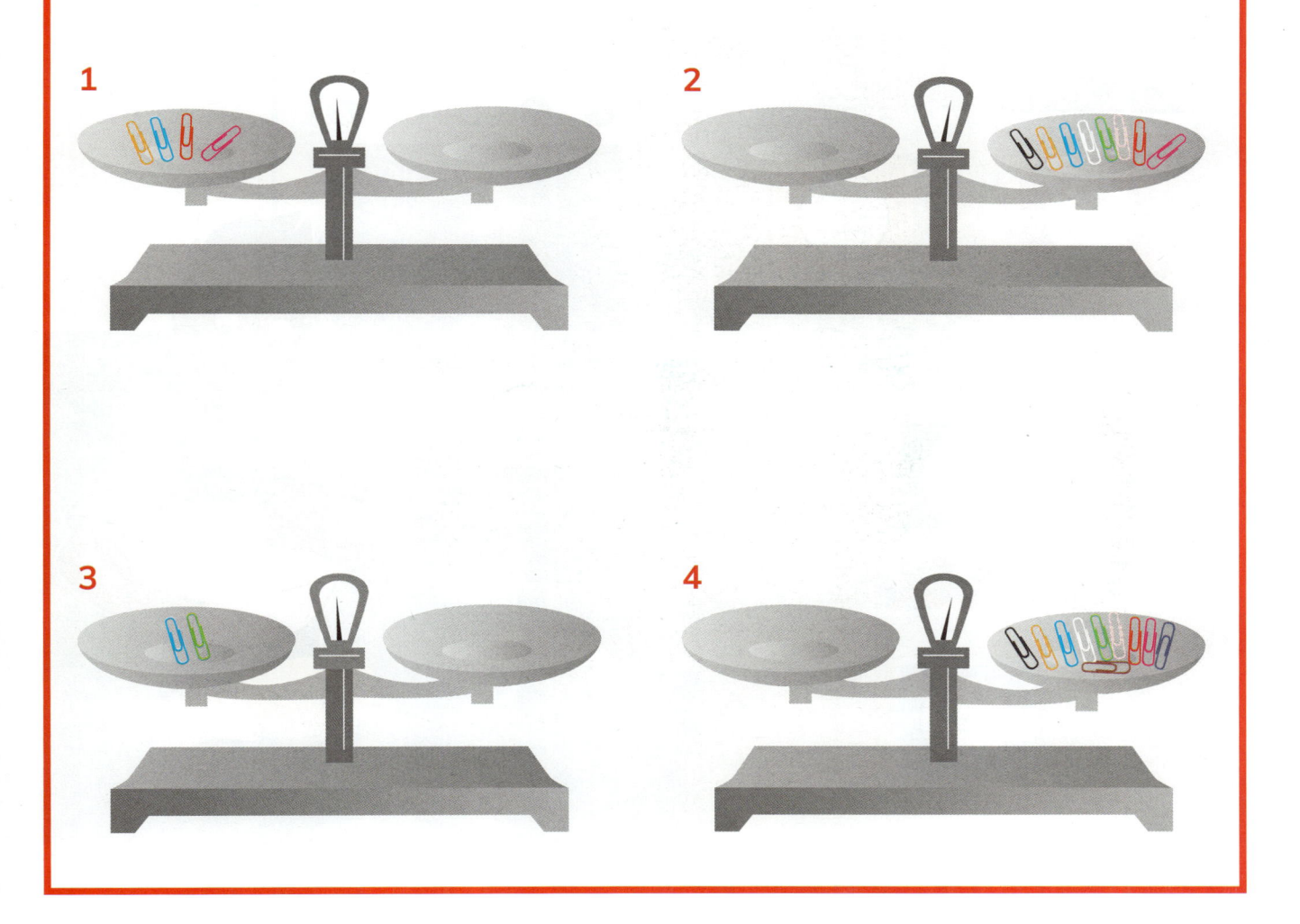

1

2

3

4

193

13 Measures (2)

This unit is about measuring mass, temperature and capacity. Mass does not depend on size. There can be large light objects and small heavy objects. We need to know how heavy or light something is if we want to move it.

Temperature is something we feel. We choose our clothes at different times in the year so we don't get too hot or cold. We bake using the right temperature for the cake. We measure temperature with a thermometer.

Capacity is about how much space there is that can hold something. A bucket can hold more water than a glass. A swimming pool can hold more water than a bucket.

> 13.1 Mass and temperature

We are going to ...

- use grams and kilograms for measuring mass
- read scales using grams, kilograms and temperature
- estimate the mass of familiar objects.

The mass of a light object such as a pencil is measured in grams. A heavier object such as a bag of flour is measured in kilograms. Light things are not always small. Big things are not always heavy.

This balloon is big and light.

We can measure temperature using a thermometer. The hotter something is, the higher up the scale the colour inside it goes.

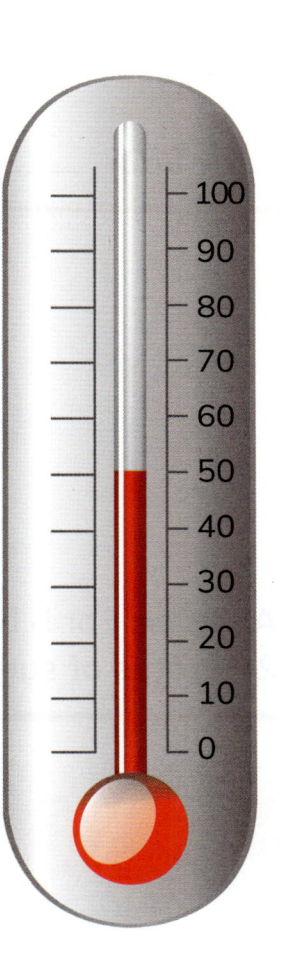

gram   kilogram   mass

195

13 Measures (2)

Exercise 13.1

> **Worked example 1**
>
> This recipe makes 10 biscuits.
>
> 100 grams flour
> 50 grams sugar
> 50 grams butter
>
> How much of each would you need if you wanted to make 5 biscuits?
>
> ____ flour ____ sugar ____ butter
>
> *5 is half of 10 so we need to halve the amount of flour, sugar and butter.*
>
> **Answer:** For 5 biscuits we need 50 grams of flour, 25 grams of sugar and 25 grams of butter.

13.1 Mass and temperature

1   The recipe for 12 chocolate chip cookies is

   100 grams flour
   40 grams butter
   30 grams sugar
   20 grams chocolate chips

   How much of each would you need if you wanted to make 6 biscuits?

   _____ flour _____ butter _____ sugar

   _____ chocolate chips

   Tell your partner how you worked out your answers.

2   Estimate and record the mass of four objects in your classroom.
    Use weighing scales and record in the table below.

Object	Estimate	Mass	More or less than 100 grams

3   Work with a partner.

    You will need balance scales.

    Use the weights on your table.

    Estimate and then find 2 weights that equal 1 kilogram _____ + _____

    Find 3 weights that equal 20 grams _____ + _____ + _____

    Find 4 weights that equal 20 grams _____ + _____ + _____ + _____

13 Measures (2)

4 Find the mass of an object using different non-standard units.

Keep the object you are weighing the same but change the non-standard unit each time. A non-standard unit could be counters, cubes, wooden blocks or something else.

Record your findings.

What do you notice?

Which non-standard unit was the best to use? Explain why.

Which non-standard unit was not good to use? Explain why.

Let's investigate

Play this game with a partner. You will need some mass cards.

The aim of the game is to get as close to 100 grams as you can.

1. Place the cards face down in a pile.
2. Take turns to take a card. Place it on one of the spaces by your scales.
3. Draw an arrow on the scales to match your card.
4. Take a second card. Add this to the first card and draw an arrow showing the combined mass of both cards.
   You can pick up to 4 cards, in turn.
   The player whose scales show a mass closest to 100 grams is the winner.

Do you think the same person will win every time?
Explain your reasons to your partner.

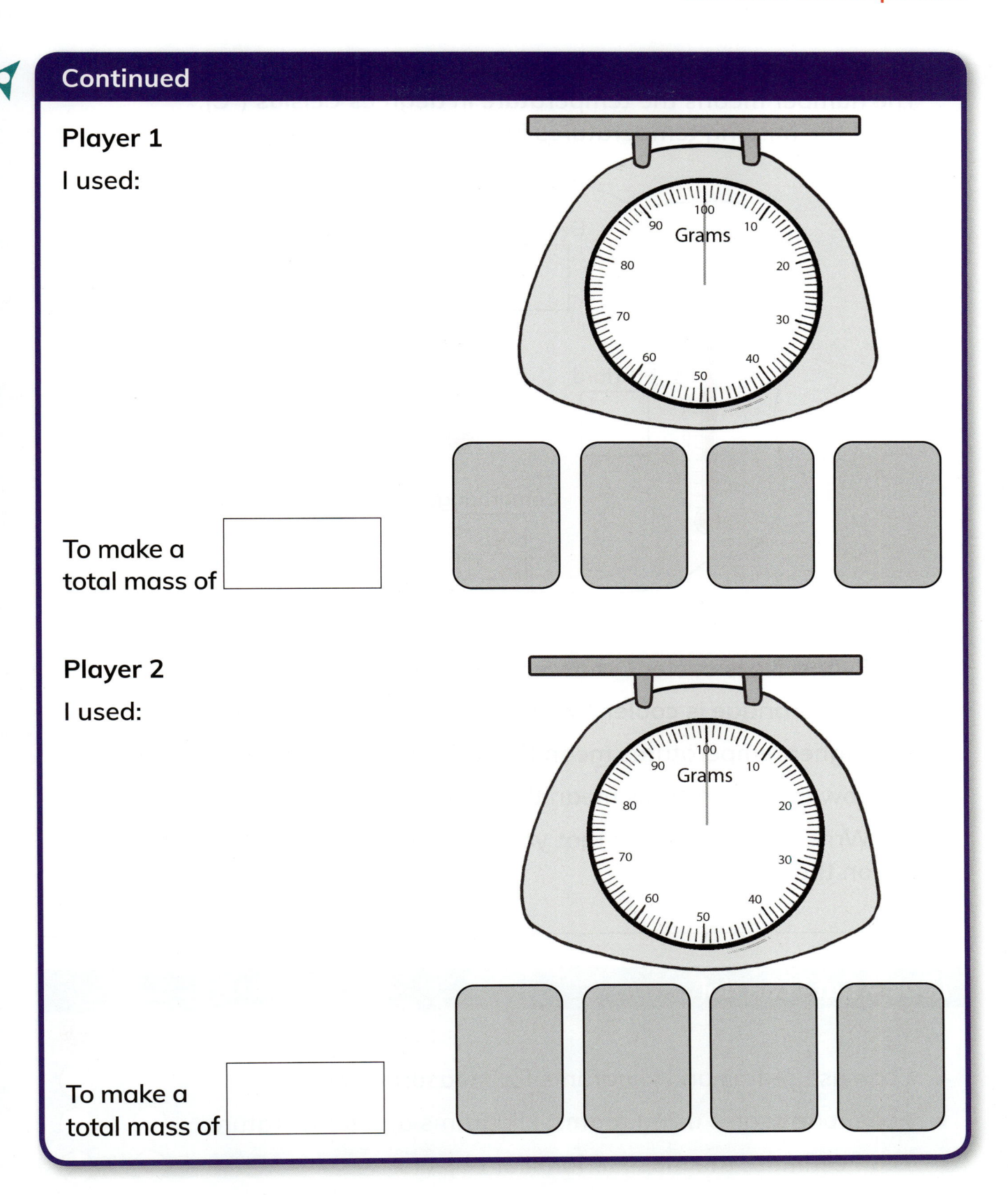

13.1 Mass and temperature

Continued

Player 1

I used:

To make a total mass of ☐

Player 2

I used:

To make a total mass of ☐

199

13 Measures (2)

5 Weather maps show temperature as a number.
The number means the temperature in degrees Celsius (°C).
Write the missing temperatures in the boxes.

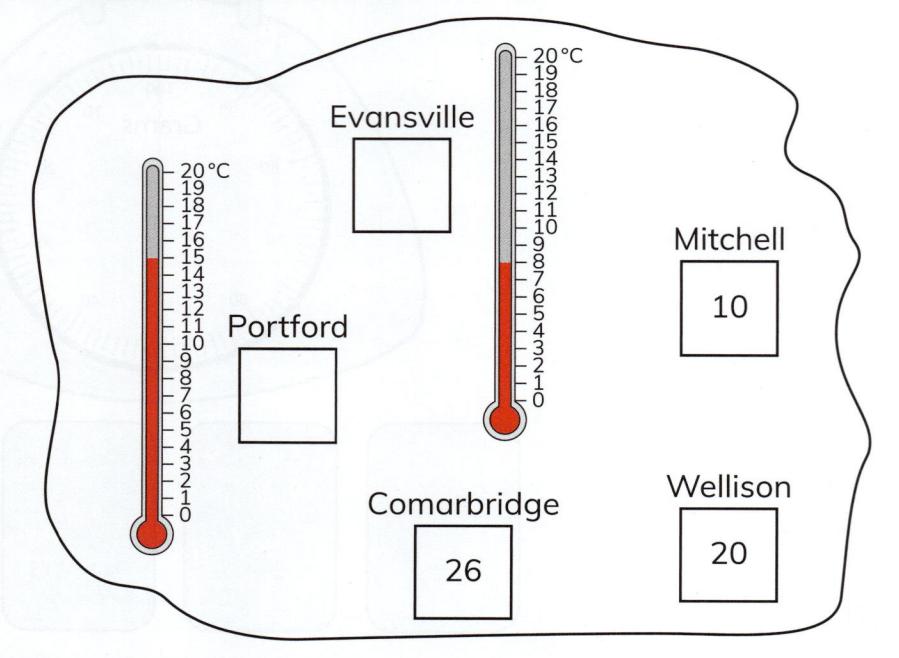

Evansville: 8
Portford: 15
Mitchell: 10
Comarbridge: 26
Wellison: 20

Draw a ring around the correct word in each sentence.

a Evansville is **cooler** / **warmer** than Comarbridge.

b Comarbridge is **cooler** / **warmer** than Portford.

c Higher temperatures mean that it is **cooler** / **warmer**.

d Lower temperatures mean that it is **cooler** / **warmer**.

e Write one other thing that you can see about the temperatures on the map.

_____

Look what I can do!

- I can use grams and kilograms for measuring mass.
- I can read scales using grams, kilograms and temperature.
- I can estimate the mass of familiar objects.

13.2 Capacity

> **We are going to ...**
> - estimate and measure capacity using standard measures
> - use litres and millilitres for measuring capacity
> - read scales using litres and millilitres.

The capacity of an object such as a jug, a bowl or a bath is measured in litres.

The larger the object, the more capacity it has.

Smaller capacities are measured using millilitres. 20 drops of water make about 1 millilitre; a teaspoon can hold about 5 millilitres.

> capacity   litre
> millilitre

13 Measures (2)

Exercise 13.2

> **Worked example 2**
>
> Estimate and record the capacity of these three jugs.
>
> —— 1 litre
>
> 1   2   3
>
> **Answer:**
>
> | Jug | More or less than 1 litre | |
> |---|---|---|
> | | Estimate | Measure |
> | 1 | more | more |
> | 2 | more | more |
> | 3 | less | less |
>
> How can we find out the capacity?
>
> There is a line on jug 2 that shows 1 litre. We can pour water into jug 2 until it reaches the 1 litre line. We can then pour the water into the other container to see if it can hold more or less.

202

13.2 Capacity

1   Work with a partner.

Estimate how much water these activities use.

Draw a line to match the activities to the amount of water.

5-minute shower		3 litres
Brushing your teeth with the tap on		80 litres
Flushing the toilet		70 litres
Filling a paddling pool		100 litres
Taking a bath		10 litres

2   Look at the capacity of the containers.
Draw a ring around the correct answer.

3 litres    1 litre    10 litres

The capacity of the tank is   15   10   litres.

The jug can hold   2   3   more litres than the bottle.

The capacity of 4 jugs is   9   12   litres.

The total capacity of all containers is   16   14   12   litres.

203

13 Measures (2)

3 Draw a ring around the correct answer.

4 litres (carton)   is more than / is less than / is the same as   three 1 litre bottles

5 litres (paint can)   is more than / is less than / is the same as   four ½ litre cups

4 litres (carton)   is more than / is less than / is the same as   three 1 litre bottles and two ½ litre cups

Write 2 more of your own.

13.2 Capacity

4 How much does each cup hold?

How much does each small jug hold?

Write a puzzle of your own.

5 Millilitres are used to measure small amounts of liquid.
Draw a ring round the objects where the capacity would be measured in millilitres.

205

13 Measures (2)

6 It takes 5 🍵 to fill a 1-litre jug.

How many 🍵 will it take to fill a 2-litre jug? _____

What about a 3-litre jug? _____

What about a 4-litre jug? _____

What do you notice about your answers?
Can you continue the pattern for 5 and 6 litre jugs?

_____

_____

7 Which sentence is wrong? Draw a cross (✗) through it.

This jug contains part way between 1 and 2 litres.

This jug contains less than 2 litres.

This jug contains less than 1 litre.

This jug contains more than 0 litres.

This jug contains more than 1 litre.

Look what I can do!		
• I can estimate and measure capacity using standard measures.	○	○
• I can use litres and millilitres for measuring capacity.	○	○
• I can read scales using litres and millilitres.	○	○

13.2 Capacity

Check your progress

1 Draw a ring around the set that holds more.

Key: 2 litres + 2 litres = 4 litres (bottle)

a) 2 litres × 4 beakers   or   4 litres bottle

b) 2 litres × 5 beakers   or   4 litres × 3 bottles

c) 2 litres × 4 beakers   or   4 litres × 3 bottles

2 Draw 2 things that you would use to measure millilitres.

207

13 Measures (2)

Continued

3   Draw the pointer on these scales.

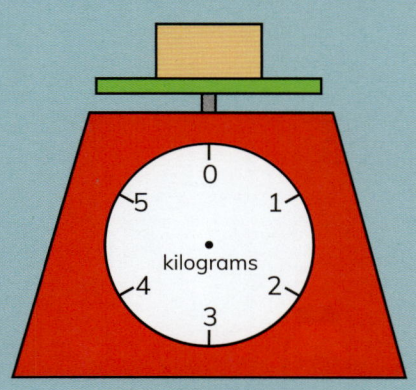

5 kilograms

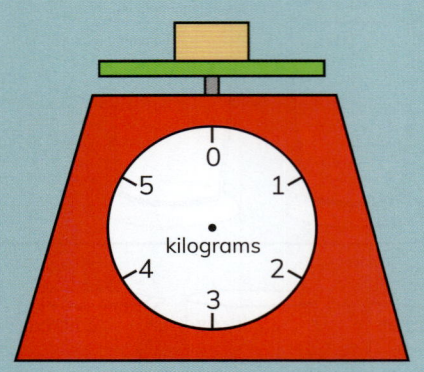

3 kilograms

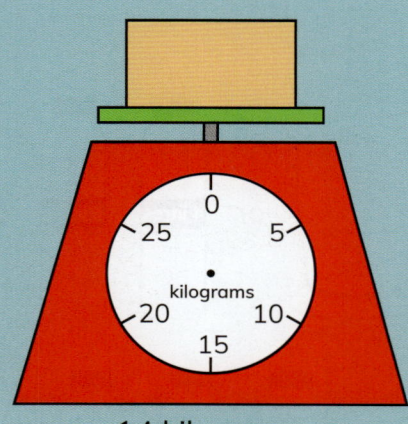

14 kilograms

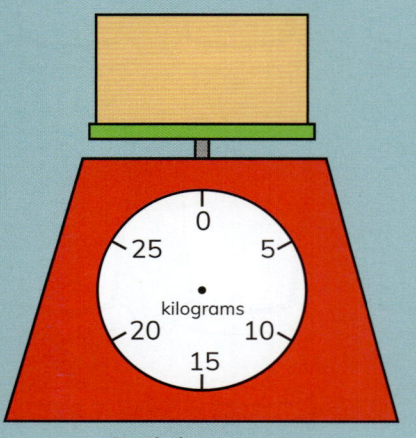

21 kilograms

4   The ingredients to make pancakes for 10 people is 4 cups of flour, 1 litre of milk and 2 eggs.

What would the ingredients be to make pancakes for 5 people?

_____

What would the ingredients be to make pancakes for 20 people?

_____

Project 6: Sorting orange juice

> Project 6

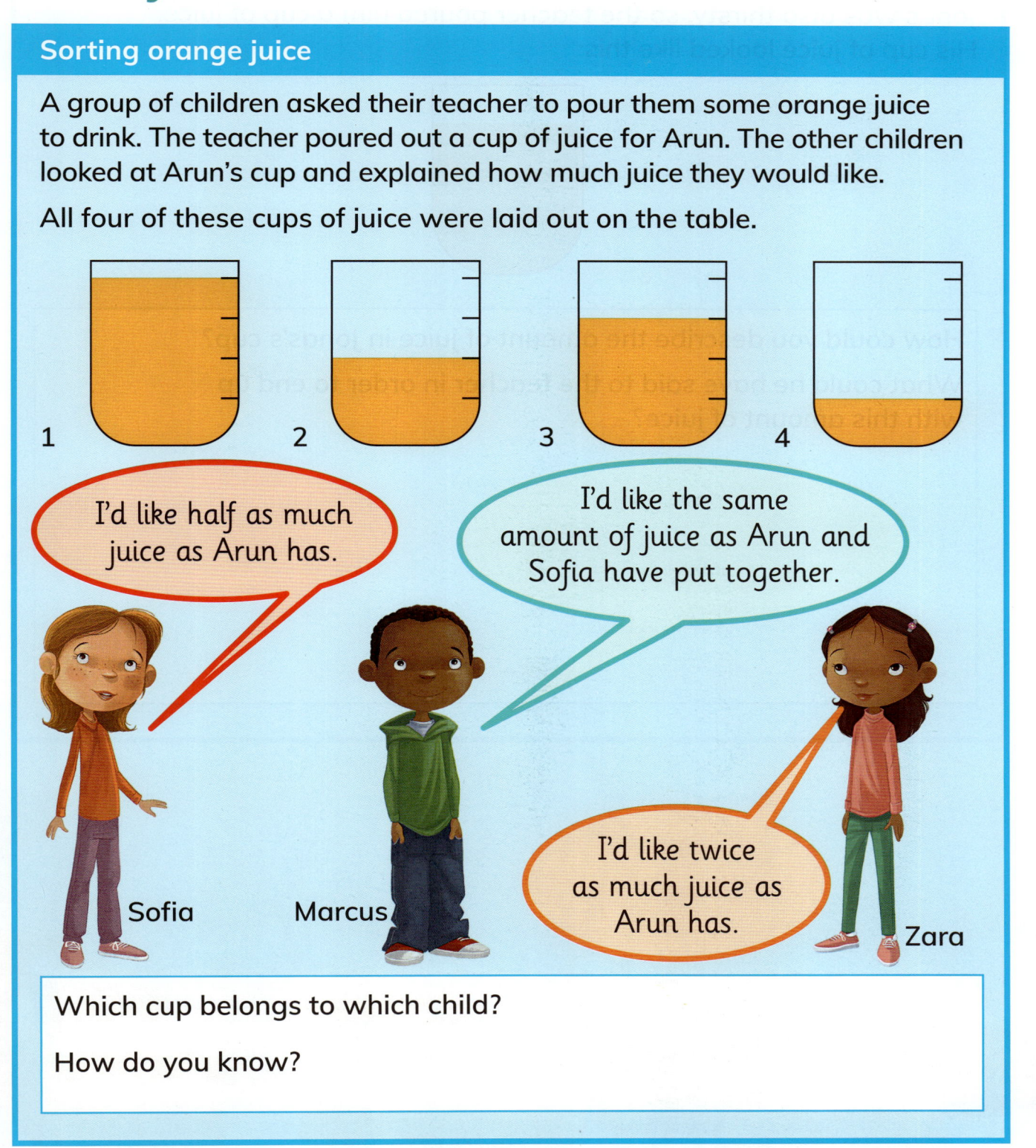

Sorting orange juice

A group of children asked their teacher to pour them some orange juice to drink. The teacher poured out a cup of juice for Arun. The other children looked at Arun's cup and explained how much juice they would like.

All four of these cups of juice were laid out on the table.

1   2   3   4

Sofia: I'd like half as much juice as Arun has.

Marcus: I'd like the same amount of juice as Arun and Sofia have put together.

Zara: I'd like twice as much juice as Arun has.

Which cup belongs to which child?

How do you know?

209

Project 6 Sorting orange juice

Continued

Jonas was also thirsty, so the teacher poured him a cup of juice. His cup of juice looked like this:

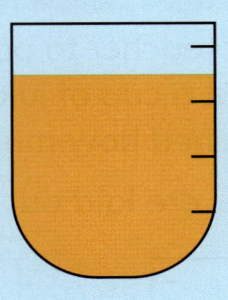

How could you describe the amount of juice in Jonas's cup?

What could he have said to the teacher in order to end up with this amount of juice?

14 Pattern and probability

Getting started

1. Use these shapes to make 2 different patterns. Draw what you have made.

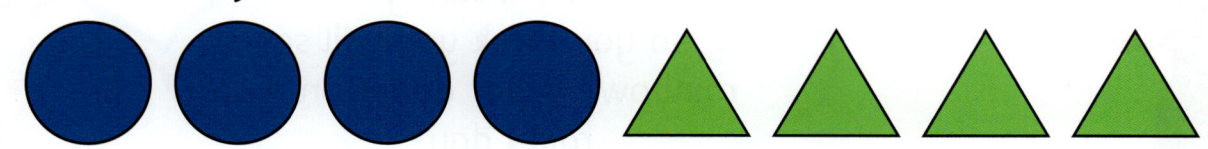

14 Pattern and probability

Patterns are everywhere. They can be found in nature, art and music as well as mathematics.

Patterns can help you say what you think will happen in the future. Probability and chance are all about patterns.

What patterns can you see in the picture?

If it's a sunny day, do you think you will see a rainbow? What about on a rainy day?

> 14.1 Pattern and probability

> **We are going to …**
> - describe regular and random patterns
> - do chance experiments and present and describe the results.

Everywhere you look you will see or hear a pattern. This may be in the sand, on a wall, under your feet or in a piece of music. You may even be wearing a pattern!

Pattern is very important because it links with all aspects of mathematics as well as other subjects.

Chance is about the probability of something happening or being true. You use it when you are making decisions such as 'What is the chance of rain today?'

This will help you to decide whether or not to take an umbrella with you.

> chance
> experiment
> outcome
> probability
> random
> regular pattern

Exercise 14.1

> **Worked example 1**
>
> Complete these regular patterns.
>
> Look at the order of the shapes.
>
> ○▲○▲○▲○
> ○▲▲○▲▲○▲
> ○▲○▲○▲○▲○▲
> ○▲▲▲○▲▲▲○
>
> *After a circle comes a triangle. After a triangle comes a circle.*
>
> *A circle is before 2 triangles. 2 triangles are after a circle.*

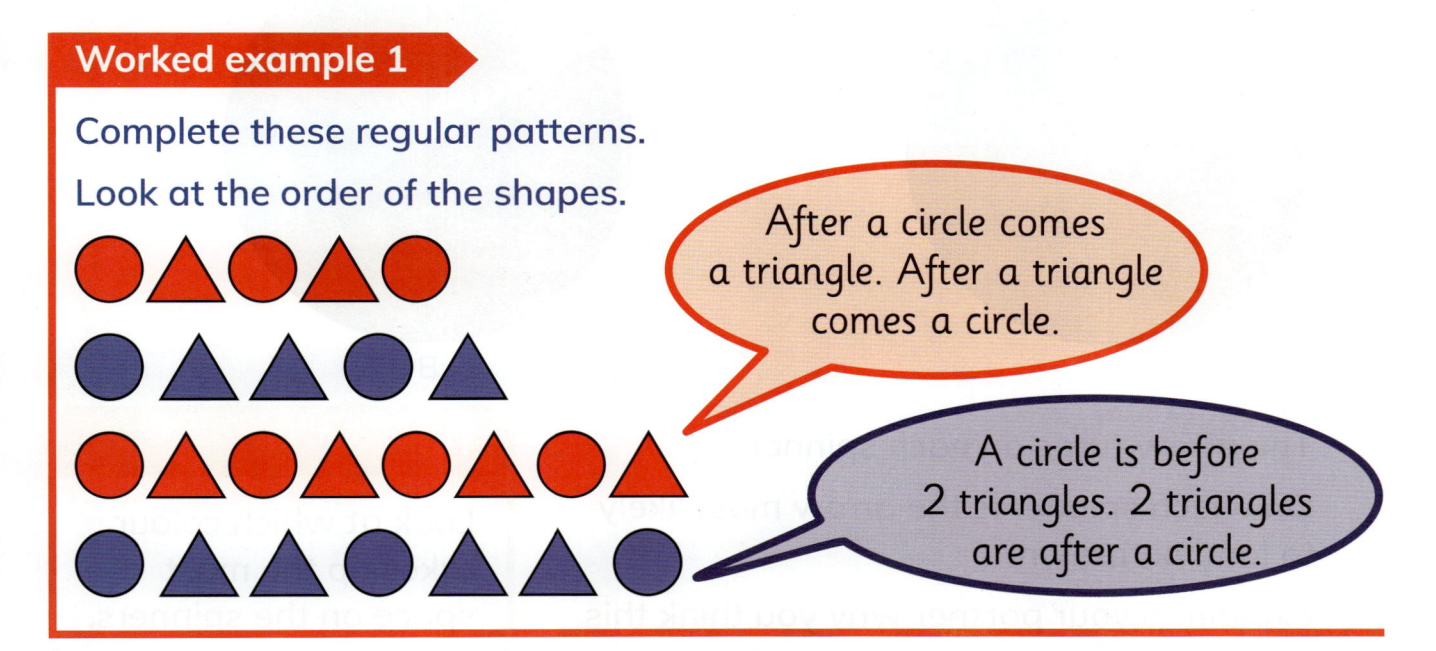

14 Pattern and probability

1 If the patterns are regular, complete them.

If they are random, draw a ring around them.

Discuss your choices with your partner.

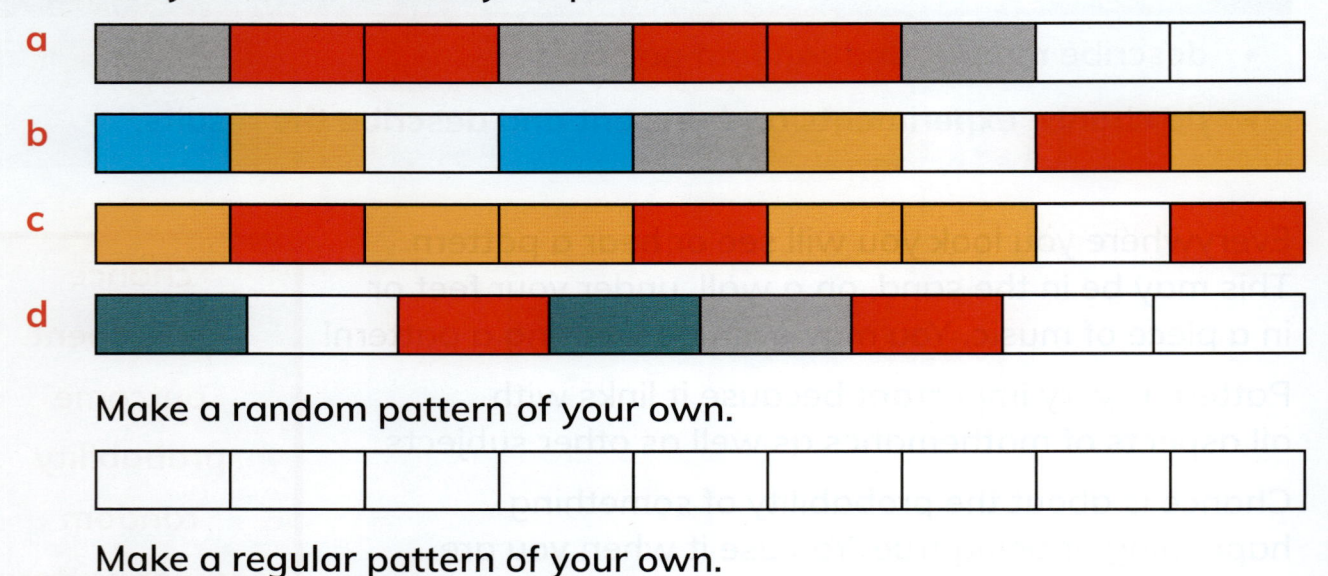

a

b

c

d

Make a random pattern of your own.

Make a regular pattern of your own.

Describe your patterns to your partner.

2

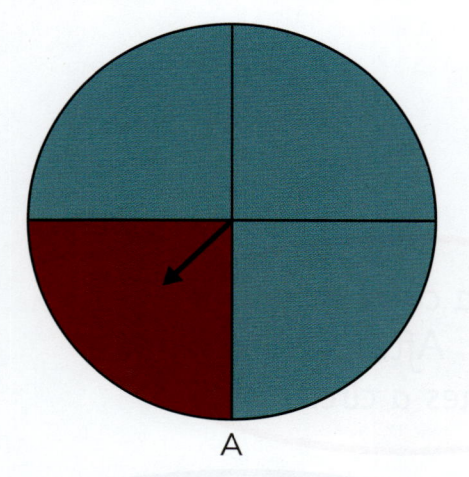

A

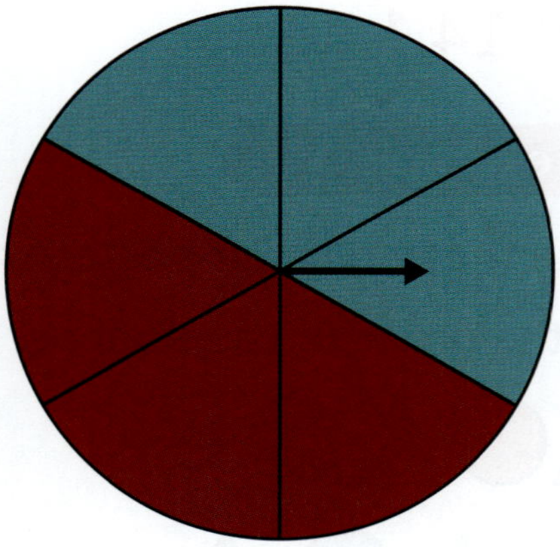

B

The arrow turns on each spinner.

On which spinner is the arrow most likely to land on brown?

Explain to your partner why you think this.

Tip

Look at which colour takes up the most space on the spinners.

14.1 Pattern and probability

3   Work with a partner. You will need a coin.

If you each toss the coin 5 times, what do you think the results will be?

Say what you think the result will be before you toss the coin.

Complete the table as you play.

Coin toss	Guess (heads/tails)	Results (heads/tails)
1		
2		
3		
4		
5		
6		
7		
8		
9		
10		

How good were your guesses?

If you tossed the coin 20 times, do you think the result would be the same? Discuss this with your partner.

14 Pattern and probability

4 Work with a partner.

You will need digit cards 0–9.

1. Shuffle the cards and turn them face down in a pile on the table in front of you.
2. Player 1 turns the top card over and places it on the table so that it can be seen.
3. Player 2 must say if the next card turned will be higher or lower than the previous one giving their reasons.
4. Keep a record of what you said would happen and what actually happened.
5. Play continues until the last card is turned.

How many of your guesses were true?

I think it will be lower because . . .

I think it will be higher because . . .

14.1 Pattern and probability

Let's investigate

Work with a partner. Use a pencil to hold a paperclip at the centre of the spinner.

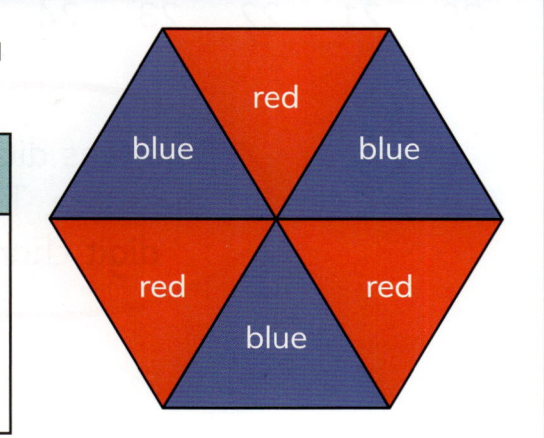

Player 1	
red	blue

Player 2	
red	blue

Take turns to spin the spinner.

Record the results as tally marks in your table.

After 10 spins each, look at and compare the 2 tables.

What do you notice?

Adapted from NRICH activity Tricky Track

Can you explain what happened?

14 Pattern and probability

5   Marcus is describing the pattern he can see in this number sequence:

20   21   22   23   24   25   26   27   28   29

> The tens digit stays the same. The ones digit changes.

Find, complete and describe each regular number pattern.

a   10   20   30   40   50   _____   _____   _____   _____

_____

b   15   25   35   45   55   _____   _____   _____   _____

_____

c   11   22   33   44   55   _____   _____   _____   _____

_____

_____

14.1 Pattern and probability

6 Draw 3 random patterns using red and blue squares.

How do you know they are random patterns? Tell your partner.

Draw a regular pattern using red and blue squares.

Tell your partner the difference between random and regular patterns.

7 You will need digit cards 0, 1, 2, 3, 4, 5, 6, 7, 8 and 9.

0 1 2 3 4 5 6 7 8 9

Shuffle the cards and place them face down in a row.

Turn over the first card.

Say whether you think the next card will be higher or lower.

Turn over the card to see if you were right.

Continue the game until you reach the end of the row of cards.

14 Pattern and probability

Record your experiment in the table.

Number on card	Before turning over the next card: Will the next card be higher or lower?	After turning over the next card: Was the card higher or lower?

What can you say about the results of your experiment? Talk to your partner.

Look what I can do!

- I can describe patterns.
- I can do chance experiments and present and describe the results.

14.1 Pattern and probability

Check your progress

1   Complete this regular pattern.

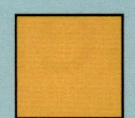

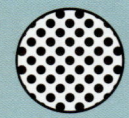

Draw a regular sequence of your own and describe it to your partner.

2   A cookie jar contains oatmeal cookies and chocolate chip cookies.

> If I close my eyes and pick a cookie from the jar, I think it will be a chocolate chip cookie.

Zara picks five cookies.
Complete the table to show the results.

Oatmeal cookies	
	1

Describe the results.

_____

_____

221

15 > Symmetry, position and movement

> **Getting started**
>
> Look at the row of learners.
>
> 1 Draw the next 2 learners at the end of the row.
>
>   Look at their arms and faces.
>
> 2 Make your own pattern using arms and faces.

15 Symmetry, position and movement

This unit covers symmetry, position and movement.

You will recognise and design your own symmetrical pictures and patterns.

You will be using words that will help you to talk about the position and direction of you, your friends or objects.

You will begin to be able to describe movement.

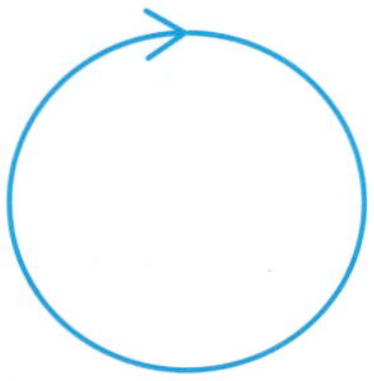

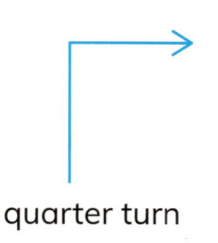

clockwise 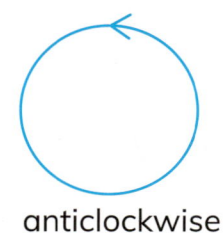   anticlockwise 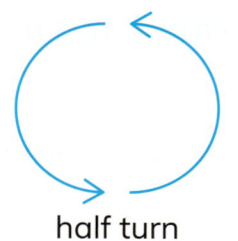   half turn   quarter turn

Follow these instructions for a dance:

| Forward two steps. Quarter turn to the right. | Forward one step. Quarter turn to the right. | Forward one step. Quarter turn to the right. Do this four times. |

15 Symmetry, position and movement

> 15.1 Symmetry, position and movement

We are going to ...
- sketch the reflection of a 2D shape
- describe movement
- use the words of position and movement.

Symmetry is when both sides of a **line of symmetry** look the same.

the line of symmetry

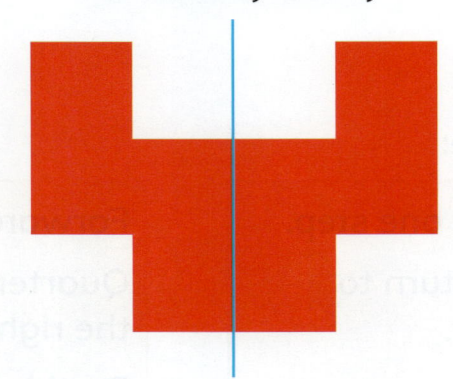

> equivalent
> mirror line
> reflection
> reverse

If you place a mirror on an object's line of symmetry, you can see the reflection in the mirror. The reflection is symmetrical.

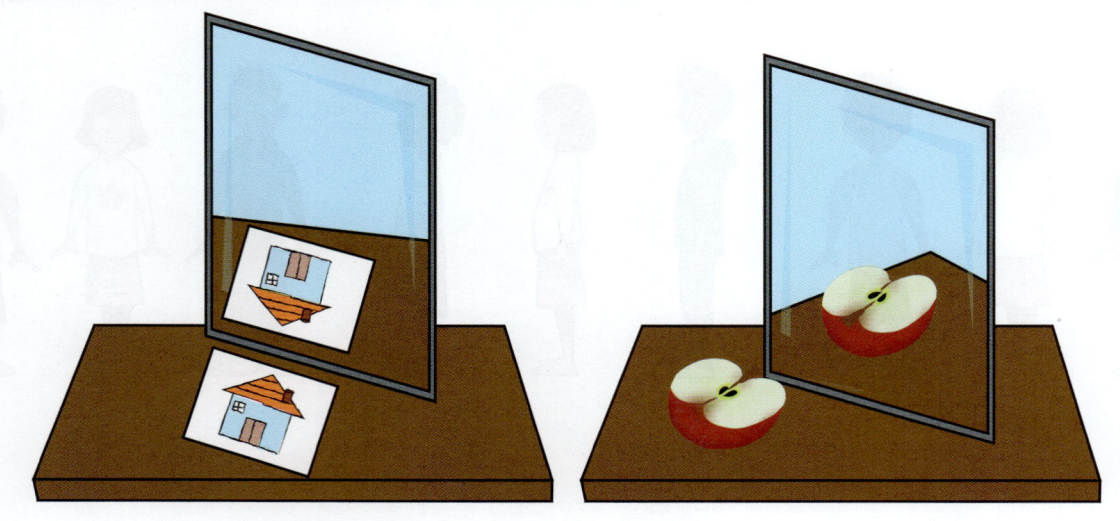

15.1 Symmetry, position and movement

Exercise 15.1

1 Sketch the other half of these symmetrical shapes.

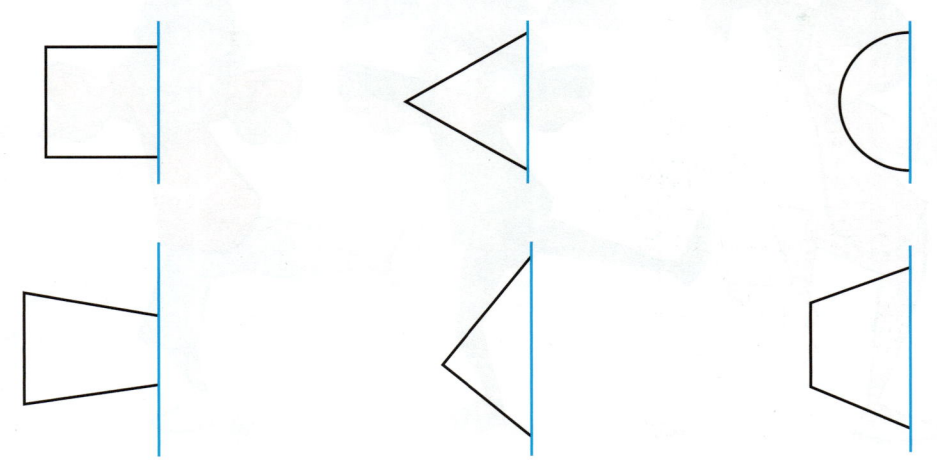

2 Look at this shape.

   Tick what it will look like when it has turned clockwise one half turn.

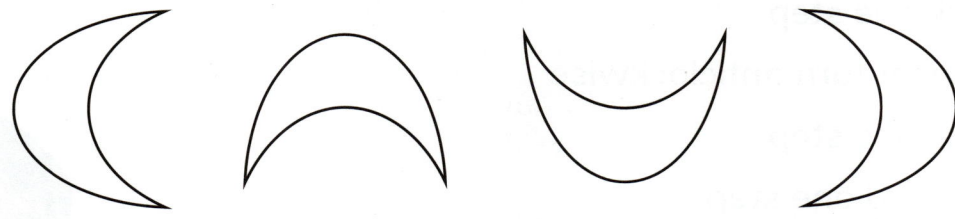

3 Write instructions to guide the tortoise
   to the lettuce.
   The first instruction has been
   done for you.

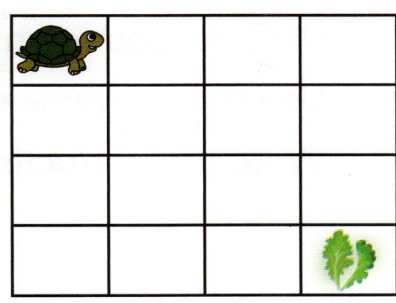

   1 Take 2 steps forwards.

   2 _____

   3 _____

   4 _____

225

15 Symmetry, position and movement

4 Work with a partner.

Follow these instructions for a dance:

1. Forward two steps
2. Quarter turn clockwise
3. Forward one step
4. Back one step
5. Quarter turn anticlockwise
6. Back one step
7. Forward one step

Make up your own dance.

Use some reverse descriptions.

Write the instructions for your dance.

> Reverse descriptions are where you do the opposite of what you just did. 'Back one step' is the reverse of 'forward one step'. You end up where you started.

15.1 Symmetry, position and movement

5   Lebeda is facing the gate.

She makes a half turn.
She is facing the pond.
Draw the pond in the correct box.

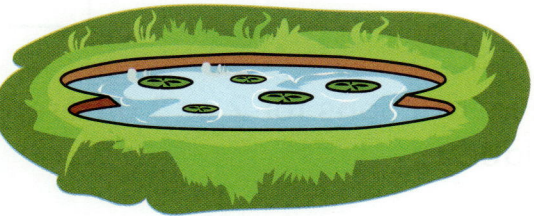

She makes a quarter turn clockwise.
She is facing the tree.
Draw the tree in the correct box.

She makes a half turn.
She is facing the tent.
Draw the tent in the correct box.

15 Symmetry, position and movement

Let's investigate

Begin at the start and follow the instructions.

1. Walk 1 square forwards
2. Make a quarter turn anticlockwise
3. Walk 2 squares forwards
4. Make a half turn clockwise
5. Walk 4 steps forwards

Where are you?

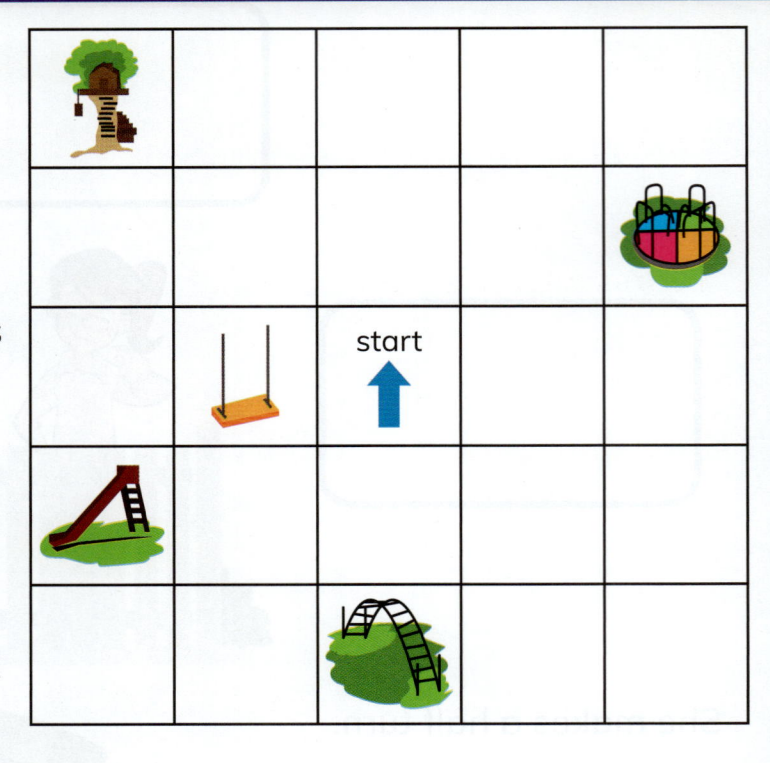

_____

Write instructions for 2 or 3 different ways to get from start to the roundabout.

_____
_____
_____
_____
_____
_____
_____

15.1 Symmetry, position and movement

> What will help you to remember the difference between left and right and forwards and backwards?

Look what I can do!

- I can sketch the reflection of a 2D shape.
- I can describe movement and use the words of position and movement.
- I can find the other half of a picture.

Check your progress

1. Draw a horizontal line of symmetry.
   Use 2 different colours to make a symmetrical pattern.

15 Symmetry, position and movement

Continued

2   Colour or pattern the last 2 cats in the row to follow the pattern.

3   This grid shows a dance. You are always facing the direction you are moving.

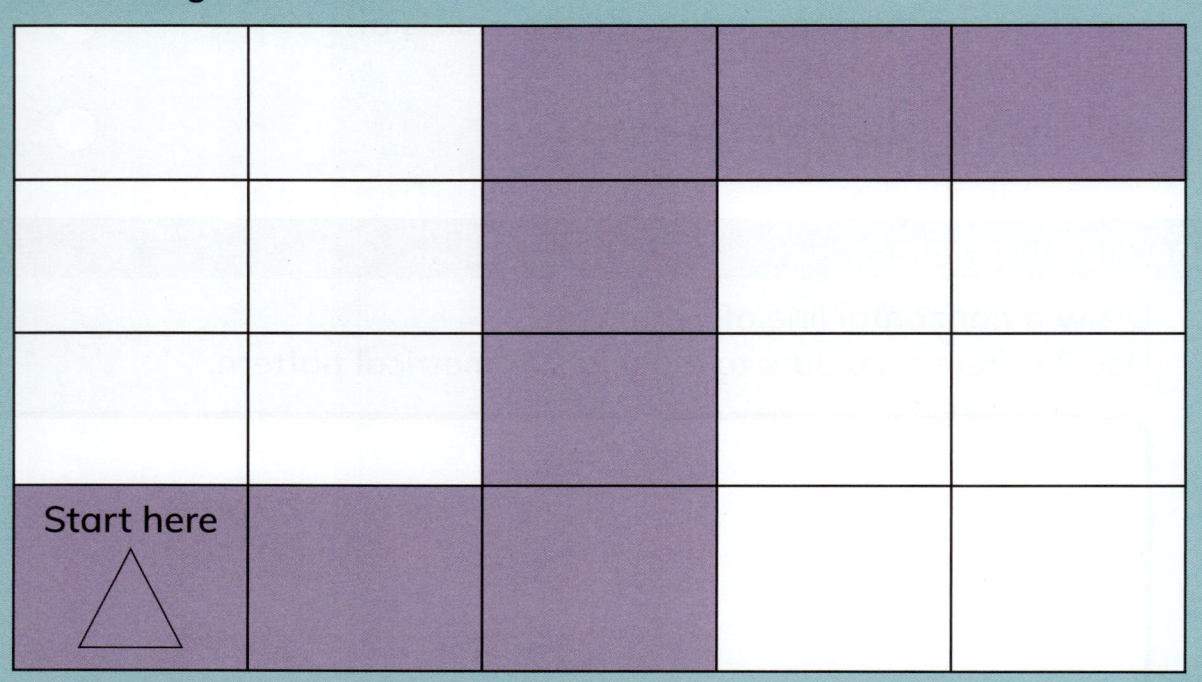

Complete the instructions for the dance.

1   Quarter turn clockwise.

2   Forward 2 steps.

3   _____

4   _____

5   _____

6   _____

Glossary

accurate, accurately	correct, without any mistakes	19
analogue clock	clock that shows the time using pointers called hands	184
angle	a measurement of turn	172
anticlockwise	in the opposite direction to the movement of the hands of a clock	172

anticlockwise

array	a regular arrangement of equal groups in an evenly spaced grid	89
calendar	an organised arrangement of the days, weeks and months, usually for 1 month or 1 year	111

capacity	the total amount that a container can hold	201
Carroll diagram	a sorting diagram using two categories	71
centimetre	a unit for measuring length	54
centre	the middle point of a shape	177
chance	the likelihood that something will happen	213
clockwise	in the direction in which the hands of a clock move	172
close, closer	near to, nearby, nearer to one object than another object	23
closest 10	another way of saying nearest 10	118

collection	a group of items	19

column	arrangement of shapes or numbers, one below another, sometimes in a grid	12

1
11
21
31
41

column addition — arrangement of numbers, placing all tens values in one column and all ones values in another column, to support the calculation — 81

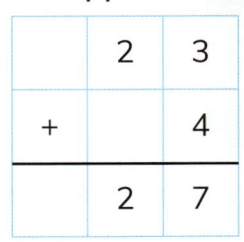

	2	3
+		4
	2	7

column subtraction — placing all tens values in one column and all ones values in another, to support the calculation — 85

	2	8
−		4
	2	4

complement (of 10, 20 and tens numbers to 100)	pairs of numbers which add to the given value. One number in the pair is the complement of the other. 10 + 90 = 100	81
currency	the units of money used in a country or region € $ £ p ¥ c	104
curved surface	the surface of a 3D shape which is not flat	31
date	a numbered day in a month and sometimes also in a year, for example, Tuesday 8th March 2021 or 8/3/2021	111
denominator	the number below the line in a fraction, which tells you how many equal parts are in the whole $\frac{1}{2}$ ← denominator showing 2 equal parts in the whole	122
digit	the numbers 0, 1, 2, 3, 4, 5, 6, 7, 8 and 9 are digits. The position of a digit gives its value. For example, in the 2-digit number 42, the 2 has a value of 2 ones, and the 4 has a value of 4 tens. 4 0 + 2 = 4 2	12

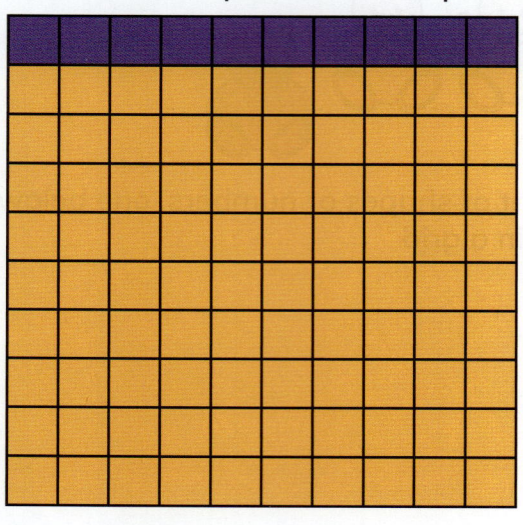

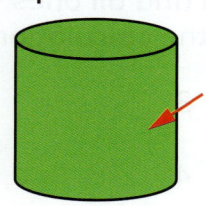

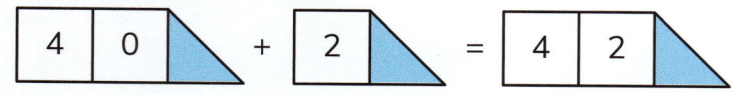

digital clock	a clock that shows the time in numbers only	184
distance	the length of space between two things	54
division, divide	the mathematical operation shown using ÷ Division can be grouping or sharing. We divide when we carry out division.	94
division as grouping	splitting the whole into equal groups 10 ÷ 2 = 5	94
division as sharing	splitting the whole by giving 1 to each person or object repeatedly until all objects or numbers are allocated 10 ÷ 2 = 5	94

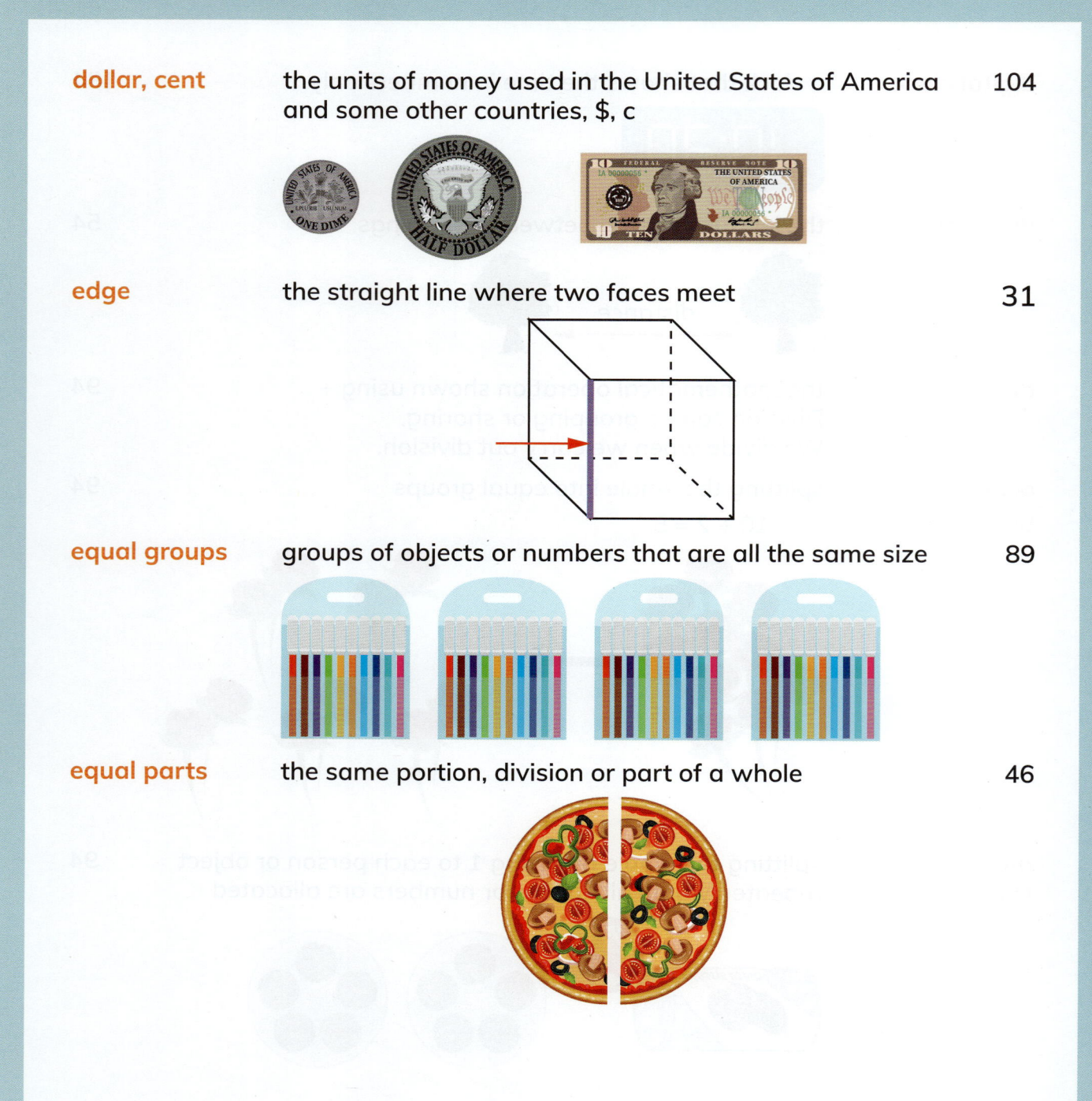

dollar, cent	the units of money used in the United States of America and some other countries, $, c	104

edge	the straight line where two faces meet	31

equal groups	groups of objects or numbers that are all the same size	89

equal parts	the same portion, division or part of a whole	46

equivalent	when two (or more) calculations or numbers have the same value, for example 12 + 13 and 11 + 14, they can be joined by the equals sign. Both sides of the equals sign have the same value.	224

12 + 13 = 11 + 14

estimate	a sensible guess, using what you know	54
euro, euro cent	the units of money used in some European countries, €, c	104
experiment	a test done to learn or discover if something is true or not true	213
extend a sequence	make longer or continue. For example, write or say the next three numbers in the sequence, 2, 4, 6, 8, 10	23

2, 4, 6, 8, 10, 12, 14, 16

face	a flat surface on a 3D shape	31

fact family	the family of calculations which all use the same three numbers, for example, 2 + 3 = 5, 5 = 2 + 3, 3 + 2 = 5, 5 = 3 + 2, 5 − 3 = 2, 2 = 5 − 3, 5 − 2 = 3, 3 = 5 − 2	154
fraction	a part of a whole, for example $\frac{1}{2}$ and $\frac{1}{4}$	46

$\frac{1}{2}$ $\frac{1}{2}$

$\frac{1}{4}$ $\frac{1}{4}$ $\frac{1}{4}$ $\frac{1}{4}$

full turn	to move something around a fixed point until it faces the same direction again	172
gram	a unit to measure mass	195

half turn	to move something around a fixed point so that it faces the opposite direction. The movement can be clockwise or anticlockwise.	172
height	the distance from the top to the bottom of something	54

Height

hexagon	a 2D shape with 6 straight sides	36
horizontal	a line that goes across rather than up and down	36
hyphen	a mark used to join two words together	118

hyphen
thirty-seven

inverse	when one action reverses or undoes another action, they are the inverse of each other. Subtraction is the inverse of addition and addition is the inverse of subtraction.	154

inverse
15 + 12 = 27 ⟷ 27 − 12 = 15

just over	almost but over	54
just under	almost but under	54
kilogram	a unit to measure mass	195
least popular	liked or enjoyed by the fewest people	71
length	the measurement or distance of something from one end to the other or along its longest side	54
line of symmetry	imaginary line where you could fold an image so that both halves match exactly	36
litre	a unit of capacity	201
mass	the amount of matter that makes up an object. It is usually measured in grams or kilograms.	195

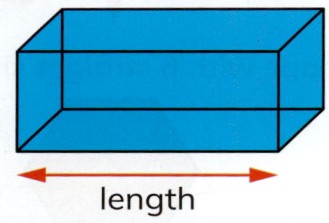

240

metre	a metric unit, equal to 100 centimetres, for measuring length	54

millilitre	a unit of capacity less than a litre	201
mirror image	the reflection of the original image	36
mirror line	imaginary line where you could fold an image or shape and have both sides match exactly	224
most popular	liked or enjoyed by most people in a group	71
multiply, times, multiplication	the mathematical operation shown using ×. Multiplication can be repeated grouping, arrays and repeated addition. We multiply when we carry out multiplication.	89

nearest 10	the tens number which a number is closest to. You look at the last digit in the number. In 41, the last digit is 1, so the number is nearer to 40 than 50. In 45, the last digit is 5. 5 is in the middle of two tens and the rule is to round 5 up to the next ten.	118

non-statistical question	has a single correct answer. For example, 'how old am I?'	71
numerator	the number above the line in a fraction, which tells you how many of the equal parts you have	122

$\frac{1}{2}$ ← the numerator in $\frac{1}{2}$ means 1 of 2 equal parts of the whole

octagon	a 2D shape with eight straight sides	36
operation	when we do something to a number. The four operations are addition (+), subtraction (−), multiplication (×) and division (÷).	85
order	a list of people, objects or numbers from first to last	19
ordering	listing numbers from smallest to greatest or greatest to smallest	23
ordinal numbers	a number used to show the position of something, for example: first 1st, second 2nd, third 3rd and so on. The first number in this list is 14.	23

Start → 14 (1st), 37 (2nd), 49 (3rd), 67 (4th), 91 (5th) ← End

outcome	a result or effect of an action or situation	213
pentagon	a five-sided flat shape with straight sides	36
place holder	0 is used as a place holder in numbers such as 40. The 4 has a value of 4 tens. Without the 0, it would become 4, which has a value of 4 ones.	12

place value grid	chart used to represent numbers in tens and ones to support understanding of a number and calculating	81

10s	1s
●●	●●●

23

polygon	a 2D shape with straight sides	36
pound, pence	the units of money used in the United Kingdom and in some other countries, £, p	104
price	how much you need to pay to buy an item. The symbol tells you which currency the price is in.	104
probability	how likely something is to happen	213
product	the result of multiplication, for example, 5 × 3 = 15	159

product
5 × 3 = 15

quarter	one of four equal parts	46
quarter past	the time when the minute hand has travelled a quarter of the way around a clock; 15 minutes past the hour quarter past 6	184
quarter to	the time when the minute hand has travelled three-quarters of the way around a clock. There is a quarter of an hour until the next o'clock time. quarter to 7	184
quarter turn	a quarter of a full turn, it can be clockwise or anticlockwise	172
quotient	the result of division, for example, 20 ÷ 5 = 4 quotient ↑ 20 ÷ 5 = 4	163
random	not following a plan or pattern	213
reflection	an image you can see in a mirror	224

| regroup | splitting a number in different ways. This is useful when doing mental maths. For example, 34 could be 3 tens and 4 ones or 2 tens and 14 ones or something else. | 118 |

→ 34

→ 34

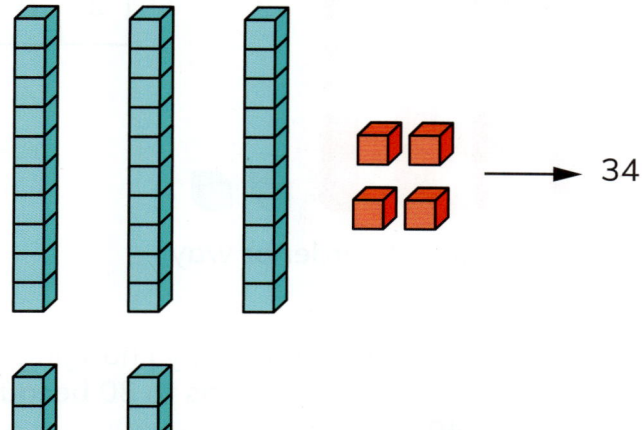

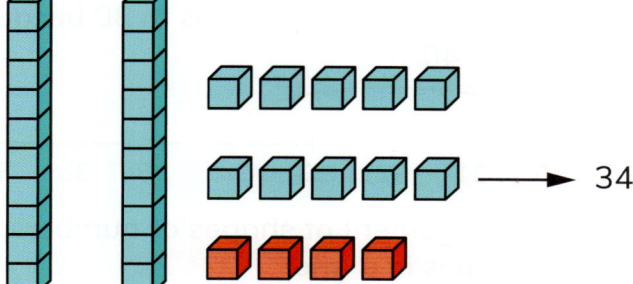

| regular pattern | a pattern that follows a rule | 213 |
| repeated addition | adding the same amount several times, especially on a number line | 89 |

$$5 + 5 + 5 + 5 + 5 + 5 = 30$$

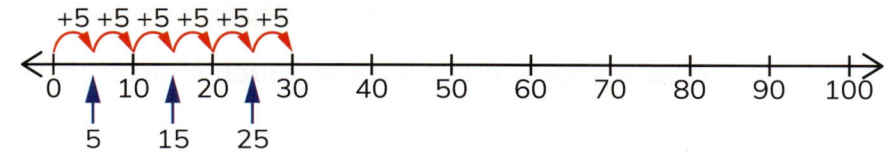

| repeated subtraction | subtracting the same amount several times, especially on a number line | 94 |

$$15 \div 5 = 3$$

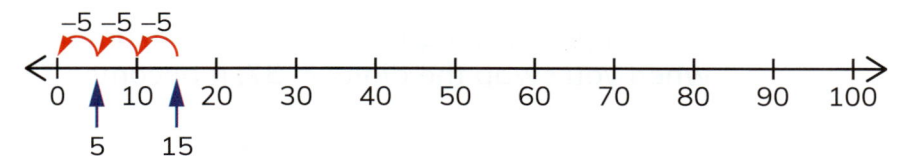

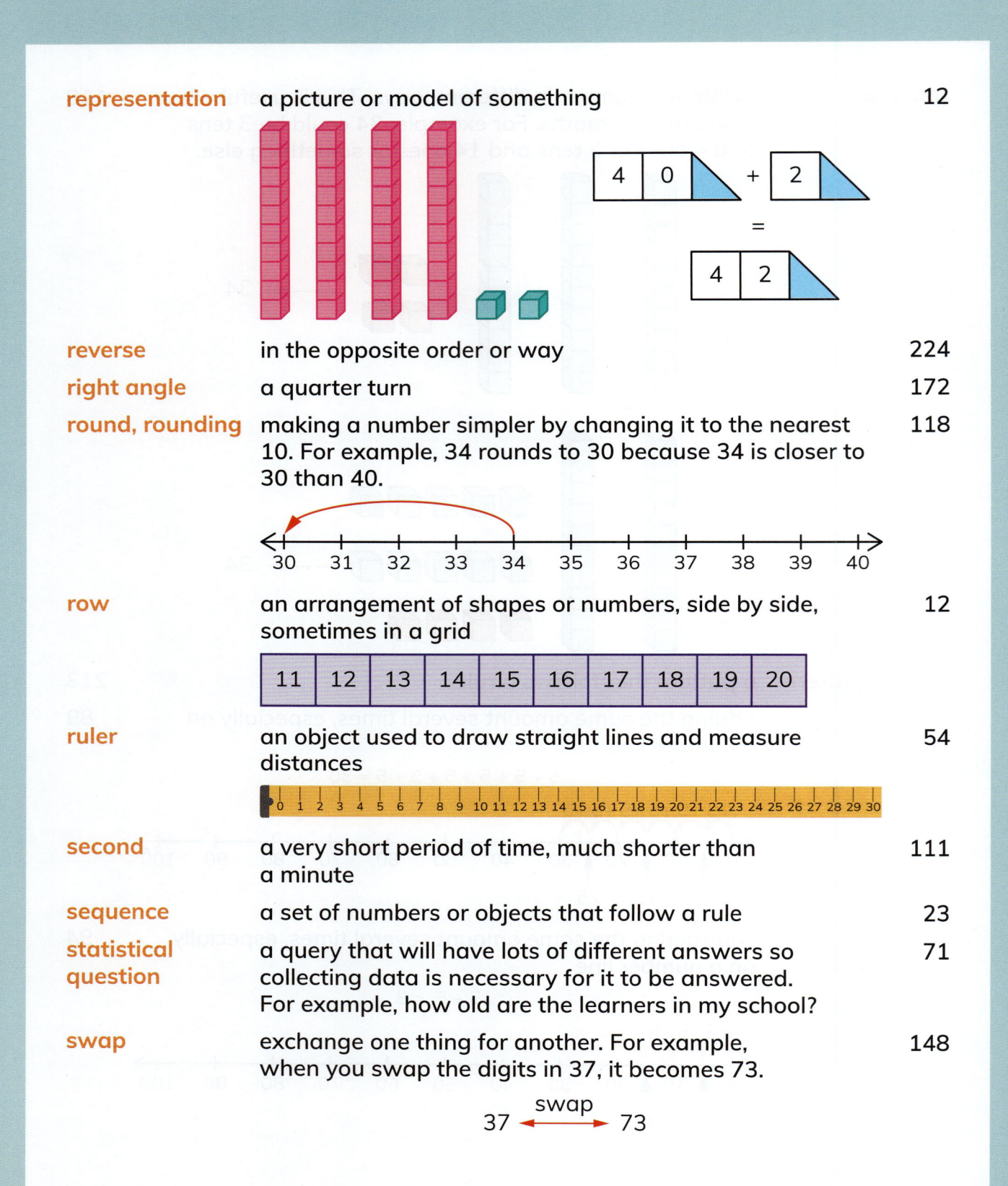

representation	a picture or model of something	12
reverse	in the opposite order or way	224
right angle	a quarter turn	172
round, rounding	making a number simpler by changing it to the nearest 10. For example, 34 rounds to 30 because 34 is closer to 30 than 40.	118
row	an arrangement of shapes or numbers, side by side, sometimes in a grid	12
ruler	an object used to draw straight lines and measure distances	54
second	a very short period of time, much shorter than a minute	111
sequence	a set of numbers or objects that follow a rule	23
statistical question	a query that will have lots of different answers so collecting data is necessary for it to be answered. For example, how old are the learners in my school?	71
swap	exchange one thing for another. For example, when you swap the digits in 37, it becomes 73.	148

symmetrical	having two halves the same where one is the mirror image of the other	36
symmetry	two parts that match exactly as in a mirror	36
tally	a record of amounts using straight lines instead of digits	71
tally chart	a uniform way of showing data using tally marks in the form of a table	71
three-quarters	three parts of a whole that has been divided into four equal parts	46
times table, multiplication table	a list of multiplication facts for a given number, usually up to 10 times that number	89

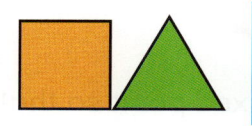

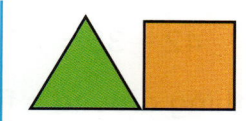

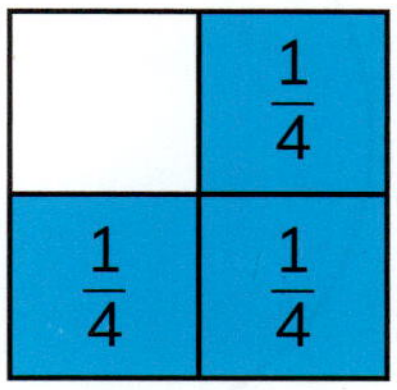

$5 \times 1 = 5$
$5 \times 2 = 10$
$5 \times 3 = 15$
$5 \times 4 = 20$
$5 \times 5 = 25$
$5 \times 6 = 30$
$5 \times 7 = 35$
$5 \times 8 = 40$
$5 \times 9 = 45$
$5 \times 10 = 50$

total	how many altogether; the answer after addition	148

$$42 + 35 = 77 \quad \text{(total)}$$

turn	to move something around a fixed point so that it faces a different direction	172
unit of money	a measure used to label money for a particular country or region	104

€ $ £ p ¥ c

units of time	the names we give to different lengths of time, for example, second, minute, hour, day, week, month, year	111
value	what something is worth; for example, the 4 in 47 has a value of 4 tens	104
Venn diagram	a diagram that uses circles to represent sets and their relationships	130

Odd — In the 5 times table

vertex, vertices	where 2 or more sides or edges meet. Vertices is the plural of vertex.	31
vertical	a line that goes up and down rather than across	36

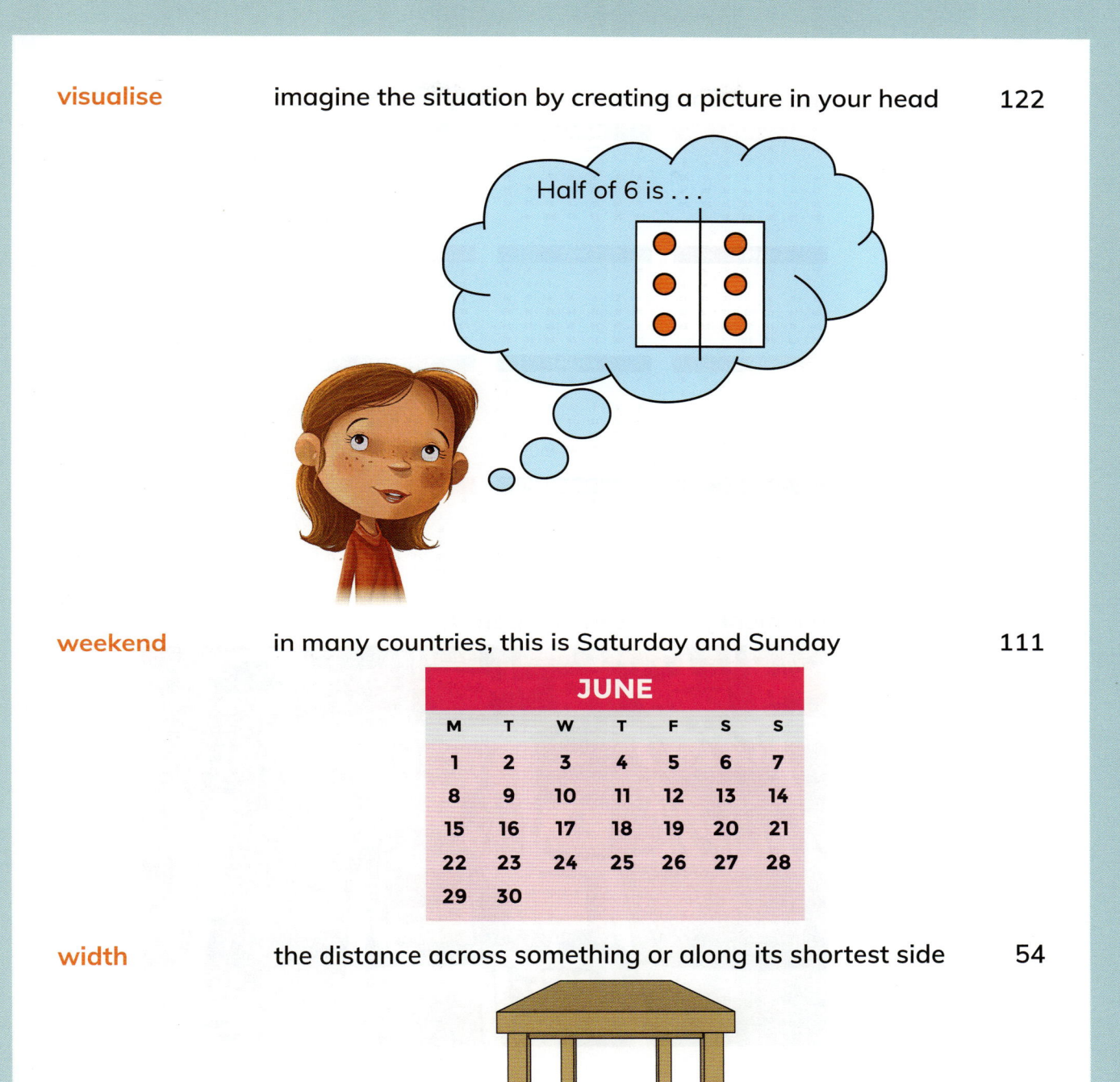

visualise	imagine the situation by creating a picture in your head	122

Half of 6 is . . .

weekend	in many countries, this is Saturday and Sunday	111

JUNE

M	T	W	T	F	S	S
1	2	3	4	5	6	7
8	9	10	11	12	13	14
15	16	17	18	19	20	21
22	23	24	25	26	27	28
29	30					

width	the distance across something or along its shortest side	54
worth	another word for value or price	104

year — the 12 months from 1st January to 31st December — 111

yen — the money unit used in Japan, ¥ — 104

250 ›

Acknowledgements

It takes an extraordinary number of people to put together a new series of resources, and their comments, support and encouragement have been really important to us. We would like to thank the following people: Philip Rees and Veronica Wastell for the support they have given the authors; Lynne McClure for her feedback and comments on early sections of the manuscript; Thomas Carter, Caroline Walton, Laura Collins, Charlotte Griggs, Gabby Martin, Elizabeth Scurfield, Berenice Howard-Smith, Jo Burling, Zohir Naciri, Emma McCrea and Eddie Rippeth as part of the team at Cambridge preparing the resources. We would also like to particularly thank all of the anonymous reviewers for their time and comments on the manuscript and as part of the endorsement process.

The authors and publishers acknowledge the following sources of copyright material and are grateful for the permissions granted. While every effort has been made, it has not always been possible to identify the sources of all the material used, or to trace all copyright holders. If any omissions are brought to our notice, we will be happy to include the appropriate acknowledgements on reprinting.

Thanks to the following for permission to reproduce images:

Cover by Pablo Gallego (Beehive Illustration); Inside: ViewStock / GI; Mohamad Faizal Ramli / GI; jyu-akc / GI; Kenneth Higgins / GI; Massimo Ravera / GI; Brian Hagiwara / GI; DNY59 / GI; burwellphotography / GI; Davor Ambreković / GI; Diane39 / GI; MileA / GI; Kyoshino / GI; Ozenli / GI; Sirikorn Thamniyom / GI; 3dgoksu / GI; Jondpatton / GI; Alxpin / GI; Nerthuz / GI; Dilok Klaisataporn / GI; Mikroman6 / GI; R.Tsubin / GI; Aleksandr Zubkov / GI; Chuck Cross / GI; DC_Colombia / GI; veronka & cia / GI; Roberto Moiola / Sysaworld / GI; Sergio Amiti / GI; Chrissy Heckman / GI; Artpartner-Images / GI; Sergio Amiti / GI; P_saranya / GI; MIXA / GI; Nico Hermann / GI; Zoom-Zoom / GI; GK Hart / Vikki Hart / GI; Jay's Photo / GI; Mohd Fildraus Halimi / GI; AlexLMX / GI; Mikroman6 / GI; AlexStar / GI; Eskay Lim / GI; Lew Robertson / GI; C Squared Studios / GI; Charlie Drevstam / GI; Westend61 / GI; Simonlong / GI

GI = Getty Images.